W9-CEK-158

THE UNOFFICIAL
NARNIA
QUIZBOOK

THE UNOFFICIAL
NARNIA
QUIZBOOK

NIGEL ROBINSON

GRAMERCY BOOKS
NEW YORK

Published by Gramercy Books, an imprint of Random House Value Publishing,
a division of Random House, Inc., New York, by arrangement with
Constable & Robinson Ltd, London
www.constablerobinson.com

Gramercy is a registered trademark and the colophon is a
trademark of Random House, Inc.

Random House
New York • Toronto • London • Sydney • Auckland
www.randomhouse.com

Printed and bound in the EU

A catalog record for this title is available from the Library of Congress.

ISBN 0-517-22800-9

10 9 8 7 6 5 4 3 2 1

Contents

Contents

Contents

Introduction

Once upon a time, a small girl called Lucy stepped into a magic wardrobe and found herself in a land of Witches and Wizards, Dwarfs and Dragons, Talking Beasts and noble Kings and Queens.

There she made best friends with a Faun, received a special gift from Father Christmas, and helped to end the great enchanted winter that had held that land under its icy spell for far too long. And it was here, of course, that she also met the Lord of the Wood, the great Lion, Aslan himself.

The name of the country Lucy found was Narnia, and the book in which she discovered that land was *The Lion, the Witch and the Wardrobe*. It was the first of the seven Chronicles of Narnia to be published, and, over the following years, six more books appeared, telling the story of Narnia from its very beginning to its last days when Aslan finally called down night upon that world.

The Lion, the Witch and the Wardrobe has been translated into many different languages, and has kept children (and their parents) spellbound for over half a century. Along with the other Chronicles, it's a classic and timeless story, and its characters are as unforgettable and as enduring as Bilbo and Frodo Baggins, Lyra Belacqua and Will Parry, or Harry Potter. If you were lucky, you might also have seen productions of *The Lion, the Witch and the Wardrobe* in the theatre, as well as on television, and now there's a spectacular film which will bring the wonder that is Narnia to a whole new audience.

The thousand questions in *The Unofficial Narnia Quizbook* are designed to test your knowledge not just of Lucy's adventures in Narnia, but of the whole history of Narnia and of all the other children from our world who were called there by Aslan.

You can read this book from cover to cover, or dip into the different sections. So if you think you know more about Shasta and Aravis than your friends do, prove it by answering correctly all the quizzes on *The Horse and His Boy* – you'll find there are at least four sets of questions and answers for each of the seven Chronicles.

Test your general knowledge of Narnia with the 'General' quizzes. Or perhaps you're confident you can find your way from the lamp-post to Cair Paravel without a map? Then see how many questions in 'Out and About in Narnia and Beyond' you can get right. And if you're sure you know all about Reepicheep, or the Kings and Queens of Archenland, then there are posers waiting for you here as well.

The Unofficial Narnia Quizbook will prove that you really are a true Friend of Narnia, and will send you back to the original books themselves, to rediscover once again that magical place which lies just beyond the wardrobe door . . .

The Questions

General / 1

1. Which character appears in all seven of the Chronicles of Narnia?

2. What were the names of the four Pevensie children who came to Narnia and became Kings and Queens?

3. What was old Professor Kirke's first name, and why did he know so much about Narnia?

4. What was the first creature Lucy met in Narnia?
   (a) A Witch
   (b) A Faun
   (c) A Beaver
   (d) A Badger

5. If you returned to Narnia after staying away for a year, why should you not be surprised if your closest Narnian friends were now very old, or even had been dead for many hundreds of years?

6. In whose house would you be likely to find Turkish Delight in abundance?

7. Which Prince was:
   (a) Put under an enchantment by a Witch?
   (b) Told about old Narnia by his nurse?
   (c) A great boxer?

8. What kind of creatures helped to plant the orchard at Cair Paravel?
   (a) Dwarfs
   (b) Moles
   (c) Centaurs
   (d) Bears

9. What was so special about the wood out of which the Wardrobe was made?

10. Name the castle that was the home of most of the Kings and Queens of Narnia.

11. Which King of Narnia was sometimes known as the Navigator?
    (a) Caspian
    (b) Tirian
    (c) Rilian
    (d) Erlian

12. How did the White Witch turn people into stone?
    (a) She spoke the Deplorable Word
    (b) She used a magic wand
    (c) She used a magic spell
    (d) She touched them

13. In what order were the seven Chronicles of Narnia published?

14. And in what order do they come in the history of Narnia?

15. On whose side did the Minotaurs fight in *The Lion, the Witch and the Wardrobe*?

16. In *Prince Caspian*, who were the Old Narnians?

17. And who were the New Narnians?

18. Who was the son of the Emperor-over-Sea?
    (a) Aslan
    (b) Tash
    (c) Father Time
    (d) King Gale

19. According to old Professor Kirke at the end of *The Lion, the Witch and the Wardrobe*, what will happen to you when you're least expecting it?

20. Where is:
    (a) Deathwater
    (b) Goldwater
    (c) Glasswater

The Lion, the Witch and the Wardrobe / 1

1. Why were Peter, Susan, Edmund and Lucy Pevensie staying at Professor Kirke's old house in the country when all their adventures in Narnia began?

2. Apart from the Wardrobe what was the only other thing that was to be found in the spare room in Professor Kirke's house?

3. Who was the very first creature Lucy met when she arrived in Narnia?

4. All the children were scared of Mrs Macready. Who was she?

5. When the Pevensie children first came to Narnia they found out that, even though it was always winter in that land, Christmas never came. Who had made it like that?

6. When they first met him, Lucy was a little scared of him, Susan thought he was an old dear, and all Edmund wanted to do was to laugh at him. Who was he?

7. Who had come to Narnia from the city of War Drobe in the land of Spare Oom?

8. Whenever she entered the Wardrobe why did Lucy always keep the door of the Wardrobe open?

9. Can you name all the Pevensie children in the order of their age, from the eldest to the youngest?

10. Lucy was the first of the Pevensie brothers and sisters to enter Narnia. Who was the second?

11. According to an old rhyme, when Aslan roared what would come to an end?

12. When she entered the Wardrobe for the first time, Lucy felt something crunching beneath her feet. She supposed it must be moth-balls. What was it really?

13. Who called herself Queen of Narnia and Empress of the Lone Islands?

14. When she came to Narnia for the first time, Lucy made her way towards a light she saw shining in the distance. What was this light?

15. Who made Lucy a delicious tea and told her tales of midnight dances?

16. What did the White Witch promise to give Edmund if he betrayed his brother and sister?

17. Who set off to meet Aslan with some loaves of bread, a packet of tea and half a dozen clean handkerchiefs?

18. Who were the Daughters of Eve and the Sons of Adam?

19. When the Pevensie children came to stay with the Professor they were looking forward to having lots of time for playing outside. On their first morning there, and on the day that Lucy discovered the Wardrobe, why did they have to stay indoors?

20. Who foolishly asked whether the White Witch could turn Aslan into stone?

Prince Caspian / 1

1. Who called the Pevensie children, Peter, Susan, Edmund and Lucy, back into Narnia?

2. Where in our world were the children when they were taken back to Narnia?

3. And which of them was going to boarding school for the very first time?

4. What was the name of Prince Caspian's wicked uncle?

5. Who was the D.L.F.?

6. Why were the Telmarine Kings so afraid of the sea?

7. Who killed Prince Caspian's father?

8. Who was the person who first told Prince Caspian tales of Old Narnia?

9. And what happened to this person?

10. When Peter, Susan, Edmund and Lucy returned to Narnia, they came across an old ruined building on a tiny island. What was it?

11. One of Prince Caspian's ancestors, King Caspian the First, was called the Conqueror. Why?

12. What is a pavender?

13. Which people lived in hiding?

14. Who was the master of the horse Destrier?

15. How did the Pevensie children learn of the story of Prince Caspian and his escape from his wicked uncle?

16. When they returned to Narnia who was the first of the Pevensie children to see Aslan?

17. Why were the Telmarines so scared to go into the Black Woods?

18. Who was Queen Prunaprismia?

19. What kind of creature was Lilygloves?

20. Name the Giant who came to help Prince Caspian.

The Voyage of the Dawn Treader / 1

1. How did Eustace arrive in the world of Narnia for the first time along with Lucy and Edmund?

2. What was the prow of the *Dawn Treader* made to look like?

3. Although Eustace didn't particularly like his cousins Lucy and Edmund, he was rather pleased they had come to stay with him in Cambridge over the summer holidays. Why?

4. What were Peter and Susan doing while Lucy and Edmund were spending their summer with Eustace?

5. In our world a whole year had passed since Lucy and Edmund had last been in Narnia. How many years had passed in Narnia?

6. Who dived off the *Dawn Treader* and into the sea to rescue Lucy, Edmund and Eustace?

7. Why did Reepicheep challenge Eustace to a duel almost as soon as the boy had arrived on board the *Dawn Treader*?

8. Name the Captain of the *Dawn Treader*.

9. Why did Caspian set off on his voyage on board the *Dawn Treader*?

10 Where did Lucy sleep when she was on board the *Dawn Treader*?

11. Who was Rhince?

12. Which of the three children kept a diary of their adventures on the *Dawn Treader*?

13. What colour was the sail of the *Dawn Treader*?

14. Which person much preferred Plumptree's Vitaminized Nerve Food to spiced wine, and was very upset when he discovered that there was none on board the *Dawn Treader*?

15. What group of islands did Brenn and Muil belong to?

16. Which other group of islands had belonged to Narnia since at least the days of the White Witch?

17. When the *Dawn Treader* arrived there, who was Governor of the Lone Islands?

18. Name two of the Lone Islands.

19. Which official only saw people between nine and ten o'clock on the second Saturday of each month unless they had an appointment?

20. Who nearly deserved his name?

Aslan / 1

1. What kind of animal was Aslan?

2. Which of the Pevensie children was the one who saw Aslan the most?

3. And on their first return to Narnia, which of them was the last to see him?

4. Who did Aslan undress on Dragon Island?

5. For most of its history Narnia was at peace. Who did Aslan call into Narnia in times of trouble?

6. How many names did Aslan have in Narnia?

7. The Queen of Underland told Jill, Eustace and Puddleglum that Aslan didn't really exist. What kind of creature did she try and convince them that Aslan was?

8. How did Aslan persuade Trumpkin that he was real?

9. From which direction did Aslan traditionally come to Narnia?

10. What were the first signs that Aslan had returned to Narnia and that the White Witch's magic was fading?

11. Who did Shift the Ape set up as a false Aslan?

12. Who did Aslan summon from his ages-long sleep to bring down night onto Narnia?

13. Which Calormene described Aslan as having eyes as bright as liquid gold?

14. Which two children did Aslan carry on his back in *The Lion, the Witch and the Wardrobe* and *Prince Caspian*?

15. What bargain did Aslan make with the White Witch to save Edmund's life?

16. Who did Aslan crown as Kings and Queens of Narnia at Cair Paravel?

17. During the history of Narnia Aslan would appear as many different creatures. In which of the Chronicles of Narnia did Aslan appear as:
    (a) An Albatross?
    (b) A Cat?
    (c) A Lamb?

18. When was the only time (as far as we know) that Aslan ever came to our world?

19. Where (and what) was Aslan's How?

20. Who killed Aslan?

General / 2

1. Name the Seven Friends of Narnia.

2. According to Mr Beaver, who or what was certainly not safe, but definitely good?

3. Who promised to treat Lucy to sardines?

4. And who gave Lucy, as well as Peter, Susan and Edmund, marmalade roll?

5. When Lucy and Edmund first returned from Narnia, Lucy noticed that Edmund looked ill. What was wrong with Edmund?

6. Which of the seven Chronicles was subtitled *The Return to Narnia*?

7. Who or what is a Tarkheena?

8. In which books do the following chapters appear?
   (a) A Parliament of Owls
   (b) The Hermit of the Southern March
   (c) Night Falls On Narnia
   (d) What Happened After Dinner
   (e) The Wonders of the Last Sea
   (f) The First Joke and Other Matters
   (g) How All Were Very Busy

9. How long did the White Witch's Winter last?
   (a) Ten years
   (b) A hundred years
   (c) A thousand years

10. Who are known as the Sons of Earth?

11. What connects (a) a black knight; (b) the Lost Prince of Narnia; and (c) the son of King Caspian the Tenth of Narnia?

12. Dryads were not an uncommon sight in Narnia. What is a Dryad?

13. And what is a Naiad?

14. In which castle would you expect to find four thrones?

15. Apart from Digory and Polly, can you name at least one other person who came from our world and into Narnia in *The Magician's Nephew*?

16. Whose ship was (a) the *Dawn Treader*; and (b) the *Splendour Hyaline*?

17. (a) Who became King after:
    (b) King Erlian of Narnia
    (c) King Miraz of Narnia
    (d) King Lune of Archenland

18. And who did the White Witch promise would be King of Narnia after her?

19. Of all the children who went to Narnia which two pretended – at separate times – that the adventures they had in Narnia were just a game?

20. Who once ran away from Narnia to the North and stayed there for many hundreds of years?

The Silver Chair / 1

1. Who were Pole and Scrubb?

2. Jill and Eustace went to a modern school for boys and girls. What was its name?

3. After his return to school after the summer holidays, everybody at school remarked how much Eustace had changed. What had happened to him in the summer holidays that had changed him so much?

4. How did Jill and Eustace try to leave our world and travel to Narnia?

5. After they left our world, Jill and Eustace didn't arrive immediately in Narnia. Where did they arrive?

6. Jill was incredibly thirsty after she and Eustace had left our world, and the only place she could find some water to quench her thirst was a running stream. Who was standing guard over the stream?

7. Who finally sent Jill and Eustace to Narnia, and how?

8. Why did Eustace arrive in Narnia much earlier than Jill?

9. Before he sailed away from Narnia, who did the King appoint as his Regent?

10. What was the task that Aslan gave to Jill and Eustace?

11. Aslan gave to Jill four signs that he said would help them in their task. What were they?

12. Name the Lost Prince of Narnia.

13. Who were the Lost Prince's mother and father?

14. Which evil creature killed the mother of the Lost Prince?

15. When he arrived in Narnia, the very first person Eustace saw was one of his oldest friends in Narnia. Why didn't Eustace recognize him?

16. Why was Jill so upset that Eustace hadn't recognized him?

17. Who came along with Jill and Eustace on their quest?

18. Why did King Caspian the Tenth decide to leave Narnia and set off on his very last journey across the sea?

19. What was the name of the river that made the boundary between the lands of Narnia and Ettinsmoor?

20. What kind of creatures lived in Ettinsmoor?

The Horse and His Boy / 1

1. Who was the Horse's Boy?

2. Whose real name was Breehy-hinny-brinny-hoohy-hah?

3. What was the name of Aravis's Horse?

4. For many years Shasta believed that a fisherman living in the south of the land of Calormen was his father. What was this fisherman's name?

5. How did Shasta become the fisherman's 'son'?

6. Name the only daughter of Kidrash Tarkaan, and the great-great-great-granddaughter of Ardeeb Tisroc.

7. Why was Shasta so relieved when he discovered that the fisherman was not his real father?

8. Why did Shasta decide to run away to Narnia?

9. How did Bree come to be working for the Tarkaan?

10. Bree met Alimash the Calormene at the fight of Zulindreh. Who was Alimash's cousin?

11. Why was it a good idea for Bree to run away to Narnia with Shasta, rather than escape on his own?

12. When they set out on their journey together which great city did Shasta and Bree first aim for?

13. Even though she didn't fight in wars, which beautiful Queen of Narnia was known as an excellent archer?

14. According to Bree what was the secret of riding well?

15. Where and how did Shasta and Aravis meet?

16. What were Aravis's reasons for wanting to escape to Narnia?

17. Before she met Shasta and Bree, Aravis had tried to kill herself. Why?

18. And who persuaded her not to?

19. How did Aravis plan her escape from her father's house?

20. Bree said it was better to live an hour in this country than in Calormen for a thousand years. Which country was he talking of?

The Magician's Nephew / 1

1. Who was the Magician?

2. And who was his Nephew?

3. Back when Sherlock Holmes still lived in Baker Street, who lived next door to Digory?

4. She called herself the Queen of the World. Who was she?

5. Why did Digory move out of the country and come to live with his Uncle Andrew in London?

6. Where did Polly create her very own smuggler's cave?

7. When Polly first met Digory, she knew that he had been crying. Why had he been crying?

8. While they were exploring the passage that linked all the houses in their street, Digory and Polly opened a door that they thought belonged to the attic of the empty house next to Digory's. What did they find there instead?

9. What was Digory's surname?

10. Who had a godmother who was one of the last people in England to have some fairy blood in her?

11. Why was Uncle Andrew so delighted when he caught Digory and Polly trespassing in his study?

12. What colour were Uncle Andrew's magic rings?

13. And what were Uncle Andrew's rings made of?

14. After Digory had told his Uncle Andrew that he and Polly didn't want to be a part of his plans, how did Uncle Andrew trick Polly into taking one of the rings?

15. When Polly disappeared from Uncle Andrew's study, how did he persuade Digory into going after Polly?

16. How did Uncle Andrew tell Digory to remember into which pocket he had put which rings?

17. What was the Wood between the Worlds?

18. When they arrived in the Wood between the Worlds, what was the very first creature Polly and Digory met there? And how had that creature got there?

19. Uncle Andrew believed that the yellow magic rings took people out of our world, and that the green ones brought people back to our world. But he wasn't quite right. Exactly what did the magic rings do?

20. After they had arrived in the Wood between the Worlds, what was the first world that Digory and Polly visited?

The Last Battle / 1

1. Where in Narnia did Shift the Ape live?

2. Shift had only one friend, who he treated more like a servant. What was his name and what kind of creature was he?

3. In the last days of Narnia, what was the good news that was brought to King Tirian and that made him so very happy?

4. Who first brought this good news to him?

5. Which seven friends returned to Narnia for the very last time in *The Last Battle*?

6. What did Shift and Puzzle find one day when they were walking along the shore of Caldron Pool?

7. And what did Puzzle think they should do with it?

8. In the last days of Narnia, if you were to meet a man dressed in a turban, carrying a scimitar instead of a sword, which land would you expect him to come from?

9. Shift was, of course, an Ape. But what kind of creature did he tell the Talking Beasts he was?

10. Name the best friend of the last King of Narnia.

11. Who was Roonwit?

12. Why did Roonwit not believe that Aslan had returned to Narnia?

13. How did King Tirian hear that the Talking Trees of Lantern Waste were being chopped down?

14. Who had ordered for these Talking Trees to be chopped down?

15. And who did the Narnians believe had ordered for the Trees to be chopped down?

16. Why did Professor Kirke call together a meeting of the Seven Friends of Narnia in our world?

17. Who set himself up as Aslan's mouthpiece?

18. Who did King Tirian call out to for help when he was tied to an oak tree?

19. King Tirian angrily accused this creature of lying like a man from Calormen. Who was he?

20. In the last days of Narnia who pretended to be Aslan?

General / 3

1. Which of the children who came to Narnia from our world was no longer a Friend of Narnia?

2. What was the name of the city of the King of Kings?

3. When they first put them on, where did the magic rings take Digory and Polly?
   (a) To Charn
   (b) To Narnia
   (c) To the Wood between the Worlds
   (d) To Archenland

4. Who said that they would rather live in an imaginary world where Aslan exists than a real one where he doesn't?
   (a) Reepicheep
   (b) Puddleglum
   (c) The White Witch

5. Can you name the very first person that each of these people met, when they left our world and arrived in the world of Narnia for the first time?
   (a) Jill
   (b) Eustace
   (c) Polly

6. Name the odd one out:
   (a) Rumblebuffin
   (b) Wimbleweather
   (c) Stonefoot
   (d) Puddleglum

7. Who made Puddleglum drunk and called him 'froggy'?

8. Which of the children from our world met a sea serpent that tried to kill them?

9. Moonwood was:
   (a) A Hare
   (b) A Mouse
   (c) A Faun
   (d) An Owl

10. In *The Lion, the Witch and the Wardrobe*, Edmund betrayed Peter, Susan and Lucy to the White Witch. Who else in the same book was also tempted to betray Lucy to the Witch, but refused?

11. On whose side were the people of the toadstools?

12. In *Prince Caspian*, who destroyed the bridge at Beruna and freed the river god?

13. What enchanted food did the White Witch offer Edmund?
    - (a) Toffees
    - (b) Turkish Delight
    - (c) Sherbet
    - (d) Cake

14. What did Reepicheep think was the honour of a Mouse?
    - (a) His whiskers
    - (b) His courage
    - (c) His tail
    - (d) His swordsmanship

15. What was the name of Digory's sick mother in *The Magician's Nephew*?

16. And what did Digory bring back from Narnia that cured her?
    - (a) A magic cordial
    - (b) Some special Narnian medicine
    - (c) An apple
    - (d) A fire-berry from the valley of the Sun

17. Which of the seven Chronicles of Narnia is the only one set entirely in the world of Narnia, and doesn't feature our world at all?

18. What do Ramandu and Coriakin have in common with each other?

19. Which of the Pevensie children was the best archer?

20. The Giants of Harfang and the Calormene people in Tashbaan both held regular festivals at which particular time of year?

The Kings and Queens of Narnia

1. What was the name of the last King of Narnia?

2. Who crowned King Frank, as well as Kings Peter and Edmund, and Queens Susan and Lucy?

3. Which King of Narnia was known as the Seafarer?

4. Which of the following was never a Queen of Narnia? (a) Prunaprismia; (b) Jadis; (c) Aravis

5. During whose reign was the Golden Age of Narnia?

6. Name the High King of Narnia.

7. This King of Narnia finally defeated the Northern Giants. What was his name?

8. What was the name of the castle of the Kings and Queens of Narnia during the Golden Age of Narnia?

9. Which King of Narnia became known as the Disenchanted?

10. What was the name of the very first Queen of Narnia?

11. This Queen of Narnia, who lived before the time of the White Witch, was so beautiful that, if she looked into a forest pool, her reflection would shine there for a year and a day. Who was she?

12. Who told Aslan that he really wasn't up for the job as King as he hadn't had any proper education?

13. What was the name of Prince Caspian's father?

14. King Tirian was seventh in descent from this King, who Jill and Eustace had once met when he had been a Prince. What was his name?

15. Which King of Narnia was also the Duke of Lantern Waste?

16. The ship of Queen Lucy and King Edmund was a magnificent galleon that had a swan's head at the prow and silken sails. What was its name?

17. Only a Human can be rightful King or Queen of Narnia. How did the White Witch pretend that she was a true Queen of Narnia?

18. Who married King Caspian the Tenth of Narnia and became Queen of Narnia?

19. And how did she die?

20. Which Queen of Narnia was given a magic cordial from Father Christmas?

The Lion, the Witch and the Wardrobe / 2

1. Who kept a picture of his father over the mantelpiece in his cave?

2. What did the White Witch do to anyone who dared to oppose or disobey her?

3. Why didn't the other children believe Lucy when she told them she had been to Narnia?

4. What was the first thing Edmund promised he would do when he was made King of Narnia?

5. What kind of creature was the servant of the White Witch who was always at her side?

6. Why did Lucy enter the Wardrobe for a second time?

7. And why did Edmund follow her in there?

8. Who was Maugrim?

9. How long did the White Witch's winter last in Narnia?

10. What was so special about the Turkish Delight that the White Witch gave Edmund?

11. Which subject did Mr Tumnus wish he'd worked at much harder at school?

12. Why?

13. After he had been to Narnia for the first time, and met Lucy there, why did Edmund pretend to Peter and Susan that he hadn't been and that he and Lucy had just been playing a game?

14. What orders had the White Witch given Mr Tumnus?

15. When she first met him, who did the White Witch think was a dwarf that had shaved off his beard?

16. After she had met him for the first time what did the Witch ask Edmund to do for her?

17. Why did old Professor Kirke think that Lucy was telling the truth and that she had been to Narnia?

18. Why did all four of the Pevensie children finally enter the Wardrobe and go to Narnia?

19. And who was the first person Lucy wanted to take them to see?

20. What kind of clothes did the Pevensies use to keep them warm in Narnia? And where did they get these clothes from?

Prince Caspian / 2

1. How many years had passed in Narnia since the Pevensie children had left?

2. And how many years had passed in our world?

3. After the death of his mother and father who looked after Prince Caspian?

4. And why did this person finally decide to kill him?

5. Into which river did the River Rush flow?

6. Which of the Pevensie children was a very good swimmer and had won medals for it at school?

7. When Peter, Susan, Edmund and Lucy returned to the treasure house of Cair Paravel, they found the Christmas presents they had been given by Father Christmas (in *The Lion, the Witch and the Wardrobe*) were still there – except for Susan's magic horn. What had happened to it?

8. What colour was Trumpkin's beard?

9. What country lay far beyond the Western Mountains?

10. And what connection did it have to Prince Caspian?

11. For many years who was Prince Caspian's only friend in his uncle's castle?

12. Who was the Lady of Peace?

13. As Peter, Susan, Edmund and Lucy travelled from Cair Paravel to Aslan's How, they had the feeling that they were being followed by someone. Who was it?

14. Professor Cornelius was in charge of Prince Caspian's education. What was so special about Professor Cornelius?

15. How did King Miraz learn of Prince Caspian's escape?

16. Who was Clodsley Shovel?

17. What kind of creature was Glenstorm?

18. Who told Peter, Susan, Edmund and Lucy about Prince Caspian and his escape from King Miraz?

19. Since the Humans had conquered Narnia all dryads and naiads had fallen into a deep sleep. Who woke them up?

20. After she was sent away when did Prince Caspian and his old nurse meet again?

The Voyage of the Dawn Treader / 2

1. Who did the Lone Islanders most often sell their slaves to?

2. On which islands belonging to Narnia might you be expected to pay for something in Calormene crescents?

3. Unlike Lucy and Edmund, Eustace had only ever been on a boat once before. Where had it been going?

4. How did Lucy cure Eustace of his seasickness on board the *Dawn Treader*?

5. Although he didn't much like mice, what sort of animals was Eustace particularly fond of?

6. Name three of the seven Lords who King Caspian sailed out to find.

7. What was the name of the slave-trader who captured Caspian and his party on Felimath?

8. Which one of Caspian's crew did the slave-trader think he could sell for two hundred crescents?

9. And which one of Caspian's crew could the slave-trader not even give away for free?

10. Which member of the *Dawn Treader* crew demanded to see the British Consul?

11. Where would you find the town of Narrowhaven?

12. The very first person the slave-trader sold was Caspian himself. He sold him for a hundred and fifty crescents. Why was the person who bought Caspian so interested in the young King?

13. How was the Governor of the Lone Islands fooled into thinking that the *Dawn Treader* was the head of a mighty sailing fleet, when really Caspian had only fifty men at his command?

14. Who did Caspian create a Duke and make the new Governor of the Lone Islands?

15. How did Eustace become a Dragon?

16. Who did the gold armband that the Dragon-Eustace wore belong to?

17. On chilly nights what did the *Dawn Treader*'s crew use as a hot-water bottle?

18. During the time Eustace spent as a Dragon, who comforted him the most?

19. Who changed Eustace back from a Dragon into a boy again?

20. And how did he do it?

The Talking Beasts of Narnia / 1

1. How did the Talking Beasts of Narnia become Talking Beasts?

2. Apart from being able to talk, in what other way were the Talking Beasts of Narnia different from the Dumb Beasts?

3. Which Talking Beast stabbed Eustace in the hand?

4. Chervy told Corin of the Calormenes' attack on Anvard. What kind of Talking Beast was Chervy?

5. What kind of creature was Fenris Ulf? (And by what name might you know him better?)

6. When he lived in Calormen, why would Bree never speak?

7. Who was the only animal from our world to become a Talking Beast?

8. What kind of animal toasted the White Witch's health when she discovered him and his friends celebrating Christmas?

9. And what did the White Witch do to him and his friends?

10. What special event did Glimfeather organize?

11. Which two Talking Beasts did Caspian create Knights of the Order of the Lion?

12. What kind of creature was Camillo?

13. Reepicheep was the first of all the Talking Mice of Narnia. Who was the Second Mouse?

14. When he saw Tash for the first time what did Ginger the Cat do?

15. What kind of creature told the Giants of Harfang not to kill him because he would be tough to eat?

16. This Talking Beast was turned into a statue by the White Witch, and, when he saw him, Edmund drew a moustache and a pair of glasses on his face. What sort of animal was he?

17. What kind of creature was Jewel?

18. Which creature was never quite himself until after sunset?

19. Who was the only Talking Beast to sail on board the *Dawn Treader*?

20. Who did Mr Beaver call the King of the Beasts?

General / 4

1. In which direction did Bree and Shasta head when they set off for Narnia?

2. One of the chapters in *The Silver Chair* is called 'The Sailing of the King'. Who was the King and where was he sailing to?

3. Who said that he told no one a story but their own?

4. When did Digory first meet Peter, Susan, Edmund and Lucy?

5. According to the Owls, how were the White Witch and the Queen of the Underland related?

6. Which two of the seven Chronicles of Narnia did C. S. Lewis first think of calling *Gnomes Under Narnia* and *Narnia and the North*?

7. In *Prince Caspian*, what did the men of Telmar believe lived in the woods near Cair Paravel?
   (a) Ghosts
   (b) Lions
   (c) Enemy soldiers
   (d) Dragons

8. Which of the following is the odd one out?
   (a) Nikabrik
   (b) Trumpkin
   (c) Poggin
   (d) Gumpas
   (e) Griffle

9. Which of the four Pevensie children was the sort who knew all about railways and railway timetables?

10. Who told so many stories about Narnia that they got balmier and balmier?

11. One of the chapters in *Prince Caspian* is called The Dwarf. Who was he?

12. Can you place the following Kings and Queens of Narnia in the order in which they reigned? King Caspian the Tenth (Prince Caspian); King Miraz; High King Peter; King Frank; King Tirian; King Caspian IX; Queen Swanwhite; the White Witch.

13. Which great hero of Narnia fought at the battle of Beruna and sailed off to the world's end?

14. Can you match up the following horses with their riders?
    Coalblack   Shasta
    Destrier   The Queen of Underland
    Strawberry Prince Rilian
    Bree   Frank the Cabby
    Snowflake   Prince Caspian

15. Who did Maugrim sarcastically call the favourite of the White Witch?

16. What present did Father Christmas give to Peter in *The Lion, the Witch and the Wardrobe*?
    (a) A dagger
    (b) A magic cordial
    (c) A shield
    (d) A harp

17. Ettinsmoor was where the Giants lived. But the Ettins were not Giants. Who or what were they?

18. Which two countries were separated by a great desert?

19. Digory and Polly used Uncle Andrew's magic rings to travel to Narnia. Many years later, who planned to use them again, this time to come to the aid of King Tirian of Narnia?

20. What did Mr Beaver think would be an unpleasant knock for the White Witch?

The Silver Chair / 2

1. What kind of animal was Glimfeather?

2. When he left our world with Jill, Eustace found himself standing on the edge of a very high cliff. What made him fall off the cliff?

3. What did Aslan tell Jill that she must say to herself first thing in the morning and last thing at night?

4. Where might you expect to meet Edith Winterblott, big Bannister and Adela Pennyfeather?

5. Who were the Marsh-wiggles and where did they mostly live?

6. After the murder of his mother, Prince Rilian would set out most days to try and track down the creature that had killed her in the north woods. But a month after her death he had almost forgotten about her. What was occupying his mind now?

7. Apart from Giants, the first people Jill, Eustace and Puddleglum met after they had left Narnia were a beautiful lady dressed in green and a silent knight in black armour. Who were they?

8. After she had met the silent black knight, Jill wondered what she would see inside his armour if she lifted up his visor. What did Puddleglum think she might see?

9. What did the Lady of the Green Kirtle send as a gift to the Giants of Harfang just in time for their Autumn Feast?

10. Drinian was one of the oldest and most loved friends of King Caspian the Tenth. Why was Caspian tempted to kill him?

11. Who organized a Parliament of Owls?

12. Why was it very important that the Parliament of Owls be held in secret?

13. Who thought Puddleglum was too full of high spirits and not serious enough?

14. Even though Prince Rilian disappeared and had not been seen for many years, the Owls at the Parliament of Owls did not believe that the Lost Prince was dead. What reason did they give?

15. What kind of homes did the Marsh-wiggles live in?

16. What kind of food was Puddleglum particularly good at catching and cooking?

17. How long had Prince Rilian been missing from Narnia?

18. Why should you always think twice before inviting a centaur to stay with you for the weekend?

19. There is a tiny stream running off the River Shribble and which runs down a shallow gorge. Why is it a very bad idea to travel down that path?

20. Who placed Prince Rilian under his enchantment?

The Horse and His Boy / 2

1. Who did the people of Calormen consider to be inexorable?

2. How much did Arsheesh want to sell Shasta to Bree's Tarkaan master for? And how much did the Tarkaan want to spend?

3. What bad habit did Bree think that he might have picked up from the dumb horses he had been living and working with for so long?

4. Bree's Tarkaan master was known as a cruel master and Bree told Shasta he would be better dead than be his slave. But he always treated Bree well. Why?

5. Name the High King of Narnia when Shasta and Bree made their escape from Calormen.

6. All Calormenes were supposed to wish for him to live for ever. Who was he?

7. When Aravis first met him, she accused Shasta of being a horse-thief and having stolen Bree. Who corrected her?

8. Why did Bree believe that no Calormenes would go near the Tombs of the Ancient Kings to the north of Tashbaan?

9. Which King and Queen of Narnia sailed to Calormen in the *Splendour Hyaline*?

10. How did Aravis and Shasta disguise themselves in Tashbaan?

11. And how did Bree and Hwin disguise themselves?

12. Anradin was a mighty Tarkaan. What part did he play in the lives of both Bree and Shasta?

13. Who was Peridan?

14. Which old friend of Aravis tried to convince her that Narnia was a land of never-ending snow and ice?

15. Why was Aravis such a good storyteller?

16. When they spotted him in Tashbaan, why did the Narnians take Shasta away from Aravis and their two Horses?

17. What was the very first creature that Shasta met in Narnia?

18. Who kidnapped Cor, the eldest son of King Lune of Archenland?

19. Who was given sugar after the taking of Teebeth?

20. What creature led Shasta through the Tombs of the Ancient Kings?

The Magician's Nephew / 2

1. Which place did Polly think was so dreamy and quiet that there was a danger of falling asleep for ever?

2. What did a duchess, a charwoman and Uncle Andrew's godmother all have in common?

3. In the Wood between the Worlds, Digory and Polly discovered hundreds of tiny pools. What would happen to you if you jumped into one of them, wearing a magic green ring?

4. What was so unusual about the sun of the world of Charn?

5. What did Digory and Polly find in the Hall of Images?

6. In the Hall of Images Digory and Polly found a square pillar. On the top of the pillar there was a golden hammer and a golden bell. There were also words on the pillar. What did the words tell the adventurous reader to do?

7. Why did Digory do what the words on the pillar told him to do, even though Polly tried to stop him?

8. And what happened next?

9. Name the distinguished person who came to London to visit Uncle Andrew and his sister.

10. Long ago, this place visited by Digory and Polly was known as the wonder of the world. What was its name?

11. What was the Deplorable Word?

12. Who spoke the Deplorable Word, and why?

13. After she had been awoken from her thousand-year sleep what was the first thing that Jadis wanted to do?

14. Before she arrived in our world, why did Jadis think that Uncle Andrew was of royal blood?

15. Although Digory and Polly never visited Felinda, Sorlois and Bramandin, these worlds all had one thing in common with the world of Charn. What was it?

16. Who pawned his watch and chain to entertain Jadis?

17. Who was Strawberry?

18. And who was Fledge?

19. Even when he was a very old man, who thought Jadis was still the most beautiful woman he had ever seen?

20. Name Uncle Andrew's sister who stood up to Jadis, and was thrown across the drawing-room by her.

The Last Battle / 2

1. Who was Ginger?

2. What did Shift suggest to Puzzle that he should do to make things right in the world again (as well as to make sure that there would be oranges and bananas at Chippingford market again)?

3. Which terrible creature had four arms and the head of a vulture?

4. After Tirian had appeared to the Seven Friends of Narnia, it was clear that the King needed their help. Why did they decide that it had to be Jill and Eustace who came to Narnia to help the King?

5. And how did they plan to travel to Narnia?

6. What kind of building had been set up on the hill in the clearing near Lantern Waste?

7. Who amazed Tirian with her path-finding skill so much that he would not have been surprised if she had had some Dryad's blood in her?

8. How did Caldron Pool get its name?

9. Before help from our world came to the last King of Narnia, who brought him something to eat and to drink?

10. Since Jill and Eustace's last trip to Narnia two hundred years had passed in Narnia. How long had passed in our world?

11. After Jill and Eustace had released King Tirian, where did they head for first of all to make their plans?

12. How did Tirian, Jill and Eustace penetrate the enemy camp by Stable Hill?

13. On their way to rescue Jewel the Unicorn, Jill very sensibly whispered to her friends to stay close to the ground so that they could 'thee' better. Jill didn't have a lisp so why did she say 'thee' instead of 'see'?

14. Who discovered who the fake Aslan really was, and also stopped King Tirian from killing him?

15. After Jill and Eustace had rescued Tirian, what did Ginger say had happened to the King?

16. Who did King Tirian send to Cair Paravel to raise an army against the tree-fellers of Lantern Waste?

17. Shift was very handy with a needle and thread. Who had taught the Ape to sew?

18. How did Shift and Puzzle know that the lion-skin they found by Caldron Pool did not belong to a Talking Lion?

19. Rilian's father was King Erlian. Where did Tirian meet his father again?

20. Who was Tashlan?

General / 5

1. What kind of creatures do all the watery things in Narnia?

2. Tarva and Alambil were:
   (a) A King and Queen of Narnia
   (b) Two stars
   (c) Two Princesses of Archenland
   (d) Two countries to the south of Narnia

3. In whose home would you expect to find:
   (a) A courtyard full of stone statues
   (b) A long room full of pictures and a suit of armour, and a green room with a harp in the corner
   (c) A cook book describing how to cook Men and Marsh-wiggles

4. The coins people use in Calormen are called crescents. What are the coins used in Narnia called?

5. Who held a Council at the Dancing Lawn?

6. What did Edmund leave behind in Narnia when he returned to our world for the last time?
   (a) His schoolbooks
   (b) His torch
   (c) His satchel
   (d) His glasses

7. Which of the following names was *never* used to describe Dwarfs?
   (a) Sons of Earth
   (b) Children of Mud
   (c) Earthmen

8. Which two events in Narnia, separated by thousands of years, did only Aslan, Digory and Polly ever see?

9. Why did the Dwarfs refuse to be taken in?

10. What effect did Eustace say the air in Narnia had on him?

11. According to Aslan, how would Jill, Eustace and Puddleglum know Prince Rilian?
    (a) Prince Rilian would tell them who he was
    (b) Prince Rilian would ask them to do something in Aslan's name
    (c) Prince Rilian would show them his ring
    (d) Prince Rilian would whisper a secret password

12. When he first met her Mr Tumnus told Lucy stories about Bacchus. Who was Bacchus, and in which book did we finally meet him?

13. Where did Eustace go on 6 August?

14. Who of the following is not one of the Seven Lords who Miraz sent off to the eastern ocean?
    (a) Rhoop
    (b) Restimar
    (c) Harpa
    (d) Revilian
    (e) Bern

15. What did Jill and Eustace discover that was bigger inside than outside?

16. Who of the following was a very bad sailor?
    (a) Lucy
    (b) Caspian
    (c) Edmund
    (d) Eustace

17. The Stone Table was where Aslan was killed by the White Witch. But what was Aslan's Table?

18. Who taught Peter and Edmund how to fight in battles?

19. What happens in Narnia every year on the first moonlit night when there is snow on the ground?

20. Who of the following was not a King of Narnia?
    (a) King Tirian
    (b) King Miraz
    (c) King Cor
    (d) King Frank

Of Witches, Wizards and Werewolves

1. What did the White Witch and Jadis, the last Queen of Charn, have in common?

2. Even though she was an evil enchantress, Jadis was not immortal. How did she gain eternal life for herself?

3. Which witch had giant's blood in her?

4. This kindly magician was also a fallen star. What was his name?

5. Who took the last Queen of Charn out for a meal in a London restaurant?

6. Jadis told Digory and Polly that she had paid a high price for a terrible secret. What was this terrible secret?

7. How did the White Witch turn people into statues?

8. What happened to the stone knife that the White Witch used to kill Aslan on the Stone Table?

9. Who, according to Mr Beaver, was the Emperor's hangman?

10. What was so special about Mrs Lefay?

11. And what did she tell Uncle Andrew to do when she died?

12. How did the Queen of Underland try to persuade Jill, Eustace, Puddleglum and Prince Rilian that there was no such thing as Narnia?

13. Who claimed that he would not die, even if he fasted for a hundred years?

14. Whose idea was it to call the White Witch back from the dead to help defeat the evil King Miraz?

15. When she awoke from her long sleep, who did Jadis mistake for a magician first of all?

16. Which of the following creatures were not on the side of the White Witch? (a) the ogres; (b) the centaurs; (c) the ettins

17. Who called herself the Chatelaine of the Lone Islands?

18. Which Prince did the Queen of Underland want to help her rule over Narnia?

19. Who killed the Werewolf at Aslan's How?

20. Which witch killed her own sister?

The Lion, the Witch and the Wardrobe / 3

1. What was the Stone Table?

2. What kind of transport did the White Witch use to get around Narnia?

3. Edmund pretended that he had never been to Narnia before. When all four of the children finally arrived there, what mistake did he make that proved he really had been there?

4. Who would always wonder what they taught them at those schools?

5. Why was Mr Tumnus placed under arrest by the Chief of the White Witch's Secret Police?

6. Even though he had never met a Faun in his life, why did Edmund tell Peter, Susan and Lucy that you should never believe what Fauns say?

7. Who believed that some of the Trees in the Wood were on the side of the White Witch?

8. Why did the White Witch not kill Edmund when she first met him?

9. Which creature told the children to come further in and further in?

10. What was the very first Bird that the Pevensie children saw in Narnia?

11. And where did that Bird lead them?

12. What item of her clothing had Lucy given Mr Tumnus as a souvenir?

13. Who invited the children to tea in their tiny house by the dam?

14. The clothes that Peter, Susan, Edmund and Lucy wore to keep themselves warm in Narnia did not belong to them, and Peter was worried that they might be stealing them. What very sensible reason did Susan give to say that it wasn't stealing?

15. Who first told the children about Aslan?

16. When they first heard Aslan's name each of the Pevensie children had different feelings. Peter felt full of courage and Susan felt as though she was hearing some beautiful music. Lucy felt the way she felt on the first day of the school holidays. How did Edmund feel?

17. Who was the Lord of the whole wood?

18. When Edmund sneaked out of the Beavers' house, where did he go and why?

19. When Edmund first arrived at the Witch's House, who was guarding the entrance?

20. Whose name did the White Witch forbid Edmund and the Dwarf to mention under pain of death?

Prince Caspian / 3

1. Who rescued Prince Caspian after he had fallen from his horse escaping from his evil uncle?

2. And what kind of creatures were they?

3. Who did Doctor Cornelius advise Prince Caspian to flee to, after the birth of King Miraz's son?

4. Shortly before he escaped, Prince Caspian was taken by Doctor Cornelius to watch the constellations from the western tower of Miraz's castle. They would have had a better view from the tall central tower, so why did Doctor Cornelius choose this smaller tower?

5. On that night what did Doctor Cornelius tell Caspian?

6. Where did Prince Caspian and the Old Narnians hold their Great Council of War?

7. If the Pevensie children were to return to Narnia, the Old Narnians thought that they would appear at one of the three Ancient Places of Narnia. Can you name one of these Ancient Places?

8. Why should you never watch a Squirrel going off to get a nut?

9. What challenge did High King Peter give to King Miraz on the twenty-third day of the month Greenroof in the first year of the reign of Caspian the Tenth of Narnia?

10. And who did Peter send to issue the challenge to Miraz?

11. Who were the seven brothers of Shuddering Wood?

12. The Telmarines thought that they had originally come from Telmar. But where had their ancestors come from *before* Telmar?

13. Who was Miss Prizzle?

14. What two friends did Nikabrik bring to the Council of War at Aslan's How?

15. And who from the far-off past of Narnia did he think could help them defeat the forces of King Miraz?

16. Who were the Lords Glozelle and Sopesian?

17. Trumpkin was a Red Dwarf. What kind of dwarf was Nikabrik?

18. Who proved themselves to be a better archer than Trumpkin in a shooting match?

19. Aslan saved from dying which one of Prince Caspian's oldest friends?

20. To save Narnia from any further bloodshed who did High King Peter call to hand-to-hand combat?

The Voyage of the Dawn Treader / 3

1. What – it was generally agreed – helped to improve Eustace's personality no end?

2. Who were Harold and Alberta?

3. Caspian called the next island the *Dawn Treader* visited after the Lone Islands Goldwater. Why?

4. And why did Reepicheep rename it Deathwater?

5. Which of the seven missing Lords did the crew of the *Dawn Treader* find on Deathwater?

6. When he had been just a small Mouse, a Dryad sang a song over Reepicheep's cradle. What did she sing about?

7. Name the magician who lived on the Island of Voices.

8. Apart from the magician, what other kind of creatures lived on the Island of Voices?

9. The loveliest story Lucy ever read was about a cup, a tree, a green hill and a sword. Where did she read this story?

10. Who uglified the Duffers or Dufflepuds?

11. And who turned them invisible?

12. Why was Lucy the only person from the crew of the *Dawn Treader* who could make the Dufflepuds visible again?

13. Who were Marjorie Preston and Anne Featherstone, and how did Lucy eavesdrop on them?

14. When she made the Dufflepuds visible, what other two creatures did Lucy make visible as well?

15. Who made and gave to the crew of the *Dawn Treader* the very first map of the Eastern Ocean showing all the islands between Galma and the Island of the Duffers?

16. What could you cure if you washed your hands in a silver basin by moonlight?

17. Who were the Thumpers?

18. It was said that the Dark Island was an island where dreams came true. Why was this not such a good thing?

19. Which of the seven Lords did the crew of the *Dawn Treader* save from the Dark Island?

20. Who destroyed the Dark Island?

Aslan / 2

1. Name Aslan's father.

2. Which great hero of Narnia sailed eastwards to Aslan's own country?

3. When the four Pevensie children returned to Narnia which of them was the first to see Aslan again?

4. Which King of Narnia did Aslan send into our world for a few minutes?

5. Aslan was killed in *The Lion, the Witch and the Wardrobe*. How was it then possible for him to come back to life?

6. Shortly after the creation of Narnia, Aslan sent Digory and Polly off into the west of Narnia. What did he command Digory to fetch back for him?

7. And why did he choose Digory for this task?

8. Who thought Aslan was more terrible than the Flaming Mountains of Lagour?

9. Which Horse, upon meeting Aslan for the very first time, thought that the Lion was so beautiful that it wouldn't be so bad being eaten by him?

10. Aslan once created a door in the air. Where did it lead?

11. Which of the Pevensie children discovered a stone Lion in the White Witch's house, and thought that the Witch had already won and turned Aslan into stone?

12. When they first came to Narnia where had it been arranged for the Pevensie children to meet up with Aslan?

13. Which creature first told the Pevensie children about Aslan?

14. Who did Aslan tell to pierce his paw with a thorn, and why?

15. Aslan was known by many names. Who dared to call him Pussums and even to shave off his great mane?

16. What was the name of the Calormene soldier who was allowed into Aslan's country?

17. What did Aslan tell Digory and Polly to do with the magic rings as soon as they returned to our world?

18. According to Aslan, what was the reason Lucy and Edmund had been brought into Narnia in the first place?

19. Who believed in Aslan, but did not think that he was an actual Lion, and was shown the error of his ways by Aslan himself?

20. Who did Aslan turn into a donkey?

The Silver Chair / 3

1. What usually happened during adventures, according to Puddleglum?

2. What kind of creatures lived in the City Ruinous many hundreds of years ago?

3. Why did the stupid Giants throw boulders at Jill, Eustace and Puddleglum?

4. The Lady of the Green Kirtle called them the Gentle Giants. Where did they live?

5. Who faced up to Carter about a rabbit, and refused to give away a secret about Spivvins?

6. Why was it important that Jill, Eustace and Puddleglum did not reach Harfang too late in the day?

7. On their journey to Harfang, Jill, Eustace and Puddleglum had to climb over the Hill of Strange Trenches. What were the Strange Trenches really?

8. Who called himself a Reshpeckobiggle, and why?

9. On her first night in Harfang, who came to Jill in a dream?

10. Why was the Giants' Porter in Harfang so surprised by the colour of Jill's, Eustace's and Puddleglum's faces?

11. What small animal was considered a delicacy by the Giants of Harfang and was a traditional part of their Autumn Feast?

12. On their second day as guests of the Gentle Giants of Harfang, Jill, Eustace and Puddleglum were enjoying a delicious meal of venison, when Puddleglum told them to stop. He had suddenly realized that they had been eating a Talking Beast. How did he know?

13. Who was the Queen of the Dark Realm?

14. Why were the words UNDER ME so important to Jill, Eustace and Puddleglum in their quest to rescue the Lost Prince?

15. What was the thing Jill, Eustace and Puddleglum discovered which was worth knowing?

16. Who did the Giant Nurse call her poppet?

17. Where could you find the pale beaches?

18. Who wanted to give Jill toys and lollipops?

19. How did Jill, Eustace and Puddleglum escape the Gentle Giants of Harfang?

20. Who was Mullugutherum?

The Horse and His Boy / 3

1. According to Bree the mountains of this country were covered in heather. Where was it?

2. Which Queen of Narnia was admired by Prince Rabadash for her great beauty?

3. Whose father was Lord of the province of Calavar and so had the right to stand with his shoes on in the presence of the Tisroc?

4. Which famous Faun, the oldest friend of Queen Lucy, travelled with the other Narnians to Calormen?

5. Should they get separated in Tashbaan, where did Bree suggest that he, Shasta, Aravis and Hywin should meet?

6. Who were Duffle, Rogin and Bricklethumb?

7. How did Prince Corin get a black eye in Tashbaan?

8. Who had High King Peter promised King Lune of Archenland he would make a knight at Cair Paravel?

9. Arriving in Tashbaan, and separated from Shasta, which old friend did Aravis meet?

10. Who was Sallowpad?

11. Why did Shasta think that the Narnians would hate Aravis and perhaps even sell her into slavery?

12. How did Aravis learn of the plans of Prince Rabadash to kidnap Queen Susan and attack Archenland?

13. Knowing that it was likely that they were being closely watched by Rabadash and his followers, how did the Narnians plan to get down undetected to their ship and escape?

14. Where might you expect to find the Hall of Pillars, the Hall of Statues and the Hall of Black Marble?

15. Who lived in the castle of Anvard in Archenland?

16. Why would taking Anvard threaten the whole of Narnia?

17. Why were only deaf and mute slaves present at the most secret meetings between the Tisroc and his subjects?

18. How did Lasareleen help Aravis to escape from Tashbaan?

19. Rabadash planned to take Queen Susan by force to be his bride. How did he then plan to appease her two brothers?

20. When Shasta asked this mysterious creature who he was he would only reply that he was 'myself'. Who was the mysterious creature?

The Magician's Nephew / 3

1. What was the Beginning of Uncle Andrew's Troubles?

2. Who decided that Jadis, far from being a mighty Empress, was, in fact, someone from the circus who was drunk?

3. When she arrived in our world what was the first thing that Jadis demanded that Uncle Andrew find for her?

4. And what did he actually get?

5. Why was Sarah, the Ketterleys' maid, having such a wonderful day?

6. Why was it so important to Digory in particular that he take Jadis away from London as soon as possible?

7. Who suggested to Jadis in London that she ought to go home for a lie-down and a cup of tea?

8. What method of transport did Jadis use when she was in London?

9. What did Jadis threaten to do to London?

10. When she arrived in our world, Jadis lost some of her magical powers. So what did she use as a weapon?

11. To save the people of London from Jadis, Digory and Polly used the magic rings to take her out of our world. Who came along with them?

12. What happened to Jadis whenever she arrived in the Wood between the Worlds?

13. After they had left London, Digory and Polly and the others arrived back in the Wood between the Worlds. Where did they go to next?

14. And who thought that they might all have fallen through a hole in the ground, which was part of the diggings for a new London Underground station?

15. Which person who came into Narnia at the very beginning smelt of cigars, brandy and good clothes?

16. When she first met Aslan, what weapon did Jadis use to attack him?

17. Of course, the weapon had no effect on Aslan and Jadis ran off into the trees in terror. What happened to the weapon that she had attacked Aslan with?

18. And why was what happened to that weapon so important for the future history of Narnia?

19. How did Uncle Andrew think he could make a fortune out of Narnia by bringing scrap metal from our world?

20. Aslan did not sing the very first song in Narnia. Who did?

Archenland

1. What country lies to the immediate north of Archenland? And which country lies to its south?

2. Ram the Great was the most famous of all the Kings of Archenland. Who were his parents?

3. How did the Tarkaan know that Shasta was probably a Narnian or someone who was born in Archenland, and not the son of a fisherman?

4. Which Prince of Archenland was known as Thunder-Fist?

5. Where in Archenland is Stormess Head? And what is it?

6. Which wise man looked after the wounded Aravis when she first arrived in Archenland?

7. Mount Pire was a great mountain on the border between Narnia and Archenland. But what had it been originally?

8. Who were Dar and Darrin?

9. When he was a boy by what name was King Cor of Archenland better known?

10. From which King of Archenland did Doctor Cornelius advise Prince Caspian to seek help?

11. What is the name of the river that divides Archenland from the deserts of the south?

12. How did Prince Corin of Archenland once very nearly come to spend the night in prison in Tashbaan?

13. A wise Centaur once predicted that Shasta would save Archenland from a deadly threat. What was this deadly threat?

14. Who was the Lapsed Bear of Stormess?

15. Who did King Lune invite to come and live with him and his sons at Anvard?

16. King Edmund once mistook Shasta for Prince Corin. Why?

17. Which King of Archenland did the castle of Anvard belong to?

18. If you were a boy in Archenland, and your brother was called Torin, what could you reasonably expect your own name to be?

19. Olvin was one of Archenland's greatest heroes. What creature did he kill?

20. Why was Prince Corin so happy that his brother, Prince Cor, had been born twenty minutes before him?

General / 6

1. Who saw the Wonders of the Last Sea?

2. During the reign of which King did Night fall on Narnia?

3. Who saved Trumpkin from drowning in the Great River?

4. And who saved Eustace from drowning in the Great Eastern Ocean?

5. The Witch who ruled over Narnia was the White Witch. What colour was the Witch who ruled over the Underland?

6. What was the name of the Lord of Victory?

7. Where did Prince Rilian say he had left half of his heart?
   (a) In Bism
   (b) In Archenland
   (c) In the Lone Islands
   (d) In Ettinsmoor

8. What happened after the Pevensie children had finished dinner with the Beavers?

9. Of all the children from our world, which appear most in the Chronicles of Narnia?

10. Which friend and adviser to King Tirian was also a gifted astrologer and reader of the stars?

11. When she saw Aslan at the end of *The Silver Chair*, the head of Experiment House had hysterics. What happened to her afterwards?
    (a) She was sent to prison
    (b) She was sent to a lunatic asylum
    (c) She was sent to the House of Commons
    (d) She was sent abroad

12. Why do you seldom see more than one Dragon in the same country?

13. Who would you expect to meet on Deadman's Hill?

14. Who was the husband of:
    (a) Queen Prunaprismia
    (b) Queen Aravis
    (c) Queen Helen

15. This wise old man had lived a hundred and nine years before he met Shasta and Aravis. Who was he?

16. What island used to lie between the Island of the Duffers and Ramandu's Island until it was destroyed?

17. Which Dwarf, and which Talking Horse, did not believe that Aslan was a real Lion until they saw him with their own eyes?

18. In which books do the following chapters appear?
    (a) The Fight at the Lamp-Post
    (b) Deeper Magic from before the Dawn of Time
    (c) Behind the Gym
    (d) Old Narnia in Danger
    (e) At the Gates of Tashbaan
    (f) The Dark Island
    (g) Through the Stable Door

19. What did Mrs Beaver want to take with her when she was running away from the White Witch, but couldn't as it was too heavy?

20. Who was the Uncle of:
    (a) Prince Caspian
    (b) Peter, Susan, Edmund and Lucy
    (c) Digory

The Last Battle / 3

1. Who did Tirian save from being taken off by the Calormenes to work in the Salt-Pits of Pugrahan?

2. Who, according to Shift, lived in the stable on Stable Hill?

3. As they set off to meet up with Roonwit, who taught Eustace the names of the Narnian plants and animals which he didn't know?

4. Her real name was Miss Plummer. What did Jill and Eustace call her?

5. Name one of the two terrible pieces of news that Farsight the Eagle brought.

6. What is Wild Fresney?

7. Even after he had rescued them from the Calormenes the Dwarfs refused to fight for Tirian. Why?

8. One of the Dwarfs, however, did agree to join the King and fight in the name of Aslan. What was his name?

9. When King Tirian revealed himself as the true King of Narnia, and called all true Narnians to fight at his side, who were the first Talking Beasts (all fifteen of them) to join him?

10. Where in Narnia did King Tirian of Narnia fight his very last battle?

11. During the Last Battle for Narnia, who released the Talking Horses to fight on the side of the King?

12. And who killed the Talking Horses?

13. After Cair Paravel had been conquered, where did King Tirian suggest Jill and Eustace go to where they would be safe?

14. Who was Emeth?

15. Rishda Tarkaan had a particularly horrible fate in store for Jewel if he captured him or if the Unicorn surrendered. What was it?

16. Who were the children of mud?

17. Emeth once spoke of a Flaming Mountain. What was its name?

18. How did Shift the Ape die?

19. How and when did Ginger the Cat lose his wits?

20. Who greeted Tirian when he went through the Stable door?

The Lion, the Witch and the Wardrobe / 4

1. Who did the White Witch tell Edmund she would make into a Duke and two Duchesses?

2. Which magnificent building had a hall with an ivory roof and an east door that looked out to sea?

3. When they discovered that Edmund had disappeared where did Peter and the others immediately want to go to find him?

4. And where did Mr and Mrs Beaver take the Pevensie children instead?

5. And how did the White Witch get to hear of their plans?

6. When Father Christmas arrived in Narnia it was a sure sign that the White Witch's power was finally breaking. What Christmas presents did he give to Peter, Susan and Lucy?

7. Why did Edmund not receive a present from Father Christmas?

8. And what presents did Father Christmas give to Mr and Mrs Beaver?

9. At the castle of Cair Paravel there were four great and empty thrones. Who were they meant for?

10. What would happen to the White Witch if anyone occupied those four empty thrones?

11 When they first met Mr Beaver, the Pevensie children were not sure whether they could trust him or not. How did Mr Beaver convince them that he was on their side?

12 When he arrived at the White Witch's house Edmund was expecting to be given more Turkish Delight. What did he get to eat and drink instead?

13 Who brought Spring, and not a thaw, to Narnia?

14 Who raised the warning when the White Witch's Wolves attacked Aslan and his party at the Stone Table?

15 How did Peter earn his spurs?

16 Why did the White Witch have a perfect right to take Edmund's life?

17. Who did Aslan call wolf's bane?

18. On whose side did the wraiths and the efreets, the sprites, the wooses and the orknies fight?

19. When the White Witch finally decided to kill Edmund, she had him tied to a boulder. Where would she have liked to have killed him?

20. If you went eastwards from the lamp-post and travelled through the wood and towards a house between two hills, where would you arrive?

Prince Caspian / 4

1. What role did Bacchus play in the liberation of Old Narnia?

2. As everyone knows, Squirrels are particularly good at slipping through enemy country but they can be very flighty. Who was the only Squirrel Nikabrik trusted?

3. Who were the first Talking Animals Trumpkin introduced Prince Caspian to?

4. After the death of King Miraz, what made the Telmarines retreat from their battle with the Old Narnians?

5. Who led the Pevensie children to Aslan's How?

6. What did Nikabrik want to do to Prince Caspian when he first met him?

7. After the Telmarines were defeated, what choice did Aslan give them?

8. In his duel with King Miraz, Peter had three marshals. Can you name two of them?

9. And which of them disgraced himself by sucking his paw all through the fight?

10. Reepicheep was very keen to be one of Peter's Marshals. Why did the High King not allow him to be a Marshal?

11. At a school halfway to Beaversdam, the maths teacher happily joined Aslan, Bacchus and their followers. What happened to the pig-like pupils she was teaching?

12. Who made Caspian a Knight of the Order of the Lion?

13. Who did Caspian appoint as his Chancellor?

14. Only a Son of Adam or a Daughter of Eve can be a King of Queen of Narnia. So how could Caspian and all his ancestors rightfully be Kings of Narnia?

15. What did Trumpkin hear between nine and ten o'clock on the morning he set off for Cair Paravel?

16. Prince Caspian thought he wasn't worthy enough to be King of Narnia. Why did Aslan think he was worthy?

17. What kind of creature was Hogglestock?

18. When Miraz became King of Narnia, he killed all the great Lords who had supported King Caspian. However he let seven Lords live. Where did he send them?

19. According to Aslan, why could Peter and Susan never come back to Narnia?

20. How did Peter, Susan, Edmund and Lucy return to our world from Narnia?

The Talking Beasts of Narnia / 2

1. What kind of animals worked for the White Witch as her secret police?

2. How did Reepicheep manage to keep his balance on board the *Dawn Treader*?

3. Who took Jill for a ride on his back and offered her a plump little Bat to eat?

4. Which animal offered Digory and Polly a supper of grass, and was surprised when Digory told him that Humans do not eat grass?

5. Not all the animals in Narnia were Talking Beasts. How did Aslan tell the Talking Beasts to treat the Dumb Beasts?

6. Who did Aslan appoint to rule over the Talking Beasts of Narnia?

7. Which animals brought Peter, Susan and Lucy to meet Aslan at the Stone Table?

8. What kind of animals were Destrier, Coalblack and Hwin? And which one of them was a Talking Beast?

9. What was so special about Fledge?

10. During the last days of Narnia, what happened to the Talking Beasts who passed to the left into Aslan's shadow?

11. Who chewed away at Aslan's bonds when he had been killed on the Stone Table by the White Witch?

12. What kind of animal was Farsight?

13. Which Talking Beast lived by the Great Waterfall in the Last Days of Narnia, and pretended to the other Talking Beasts that he was really a very old Human?

14. When they first met why did Bree and Aravis have so much to talk about?

15. What did three Mice, two Moles and one Rabbit bring to King Tirian of Narnia when he was tied to an oak tree?

16. Which animals have a hereditary right to be one of the Marshals of the List of the King of Narnia?

17. In the last days of Narnia King Tirian spotted a Water-Rat taking logs down the river on a raft. Where did the Water-Rat say he was taking the logs to?

18. Who was Pattertwig?

19. Who killed Maugrim the Wolf?

20. What was one of the most terrible things that could happen to a Talking Beast of Narnia, and which did, in fact, happen to Ginger the Cat?

General / 7

1. Name the brother of:
   (a) King Cor of Archenland
   (b) Darrin of Archenland
   (c) The High King Peter

2. On the Island of the Dufflepuds, who was Clipsie?

3. Where could you find drinkable light?

4. When he travelled to Charn, Digory saw that its sun was large and red, a sure sign that it was dying. Where and when did he see another sun that was dying?

5. Where were Peter, Susan, Edmund and Lucy when they were pulled back into Narnia for the second time?
   (a) At school
   (b) At their cousin Eustace's
   (c) At a railway station
   (d) At the seaside

6. Who did the Queen of Underland describe to Jill, Eustace and Puddleglum as gentle and courteous people?

7. Who planted the Tree of Protection in Narnia?

8. In the same story who tried to plant Uncle Andrew?

9. Who disguised themselves as:
   (a) Calormene soldiers in the final days of Narnia
   (b) Aslan
   (c) A green serpent
   (d) Peasants in Tashbaan

10. Who suggested to Peter and Susan that they should start minding their own business?

11. On their return to Narnia, and before they came to the Shadowlands, who was the one person, apart from Aslan, who Jill and Eustace recognized from their earlier trip to Narnia?

12. Which of these is not in Narnia?
    (a) Glasswater
    (b) Caldron Pool
    (c) Beaversdam
    (d) Ilkeen

13. The Sea People sang at the coronation of Kings Peter and Edmund, and Queens Susan and Lucy. When did Lucy meet another of the Sea People, who instantly became her friend, although they never said any words to each other?

14. Whose Aunt was:
    (a) Alberta
    (b) Letty
    (c) Prunaprismia

15. What in the Narnian sky is known as the Spear-Head?

16. Apart from Aslan, which other character appears in *The Lion, the Witch and the Wardrobe*, *The Horse and His Boy* and *The Last Battle*?

17. Who lived in the Shallow Lands?

18. And who came from the Really Deep Land?

19. Who believed in Aslan?
    (a) Trufflehunter
    (b) Trumpkin
    (c) Nikabrik

20. Which of the following is the odd one out?
    (a) Thornbut
    (b) Stonefoot
    (c) Griffle
    (d) Diggle

The Voyage of the Dawn Treader / 4

1. It was an Albatross who led the *Dawn Treader* away from the Dark Island and into calmer waters. Who was the Albatross really?

2. Who was Ramandu?

3. Who were the Three Sleepers who Caspian and the others discovered seated at a stone table on Ramandu's Island?

4. And why had they fallen into such a deep and enchanted sleep?

5. According to Ramandu, what was the only way that the enchantment could be broken?

6. What did a bird bring to Ramandu each morning?

7. What great gift did Ramandu give to Rhoop?

8. Ramandu had a beautiful daughter. Who did she later marry?

9. Not all the people who sailed on the *Dawn Treader* had the right to be called a Dawn Treader. According to Caspian who had that right?

10. Who was Pittencream?

11. For a while after leaving Ramandu's Island, what creatures followed the *Dawn Treader*?

12. What was the first clue that Reepicheep had that they were coming close to the end of the world?

13. Who had always dreamt of travelling to a world like ours that is round like a ball?

14. By what other name was Lily Lake known?

15. As they approached the end of the world, Caspian wanted to send the *Dawn Treader* back to Narnia, abandon the throne of Narnia, and travel on with Reepicheep, Lucy, Edmund and Eustace to the world's end. Who persuaded him to return home?

16. As the *Dawn Treader* approached the end of the world, why did Drinian tell Lucy not to tell the crew anything about the Sea People she had seen?

17. What kind of creature was waiting for Lucy, Edmund and Eustace at the end of the world?

18. Who described himself as the great Bridge Builder?

19. Which of the children did Aslan say could never return to Narnia because they were too old?

20. When he returned to our world, his parents decided that Eustace had changed and become very tiresome. Who did they blame for this?

The Silver Chair / 4

1. If you were invited to a Giants' Autumn Feast, what would you expect to eat between the fish course and the joint?

2. Why was Prince Rilian so important to the Queen of Underland's plans to invade Narnia?

3. Who were the Earthmen?

4. When Jill, Eustace and Puddleglum arrived in the Underland, where was the Queen?

5. According to the Underlanders, where do few people return to once they have descended to the Underland?

6. In a cavern in the Deep Realm, Jill, Eustace and Puddleglum discovered the sleeping body of a great king, who, so it was said, would wake up again at the very end of the world. Who was he?

7. Among the Marsh-wiggles Puddleglum had a reputation for being flighty. Who did Puddleglum think would make him take a more serious view on life?

8. In the Underland Jill, Eustace and Puddleglum met someone who they first thought was a dangerous lunatic. Who was he really?

9. Where would you find the land of Bism?

10. Every night the Prince had to be tied to the Silver Chair. According to the Queen of Underland what would happen if he was allowed to be free?

11. And what would really happen?

12. Who convinced Jill, Eustace and Puddleglum that there was no sun?

13. Who destroyed the Silver Chair?

14. How – and why – did Puddleglum burn his foot?

15. When the Witch discovered that Rilian had been defeated she turned into a green serpent to destroy them all. Who killed her?

16. At Experiment House no one called each other by their first names. When was the first time Jill and Eustace called each other by their first names?

17. After the death of the Witch the Underland fell apart. Why?

18. Jill, Eustace, Puddleglum and Rilian returned to Narnia just in time for which great annual event?

19. What was the Healing of Harms?

20. What last favour did King Caspian, Rilian's father, ask from Aslan?

The Horse and His Boy / 4

1. Who looked after Aravis and the horses while Shasta went off to warn King Lune about the coming of Rabadash and his army?

2. Even though his armies were mightier than those in Narnia, the Tisroc never tried to attack Narnia. Why?

3. Who was Shasta's unwelcome fellow traveller?

4. Why could the High King Peter not come to the help of King Lune when he was under attack from Prince Rabadash and his men?

5. The Hermit of the Southern March rarely left his hermitage. How did he learn of what was going on in the outside world?

6. Which Calormene – who Aravis especially hated – became the Grand Vizier after the death of the old Axartha?

7. What did Bree and Hwin do immediately before they entered Archenland? (Bree thought it might be the last chance they ever had of doing it.)

8. Why was Prince Corin so glad that he would never have to become King?

9. As Shasta and Aravis, Bree and Hwin, raced towards the Southern March which savage animal chased them?

10. The animal chasing them managed to scratch Aravis across the back ten times. Why ten times?

11. After reaching Archenland Bree was so ashamed of himself that he decided to return to Calormen and become a slave again. Why?

12. And who persuaded him not to?

13. What did fifty Calormenes, led by Rabadash, use to try and break down the gate of Anvard?

14. Long ago, a wise centaur had predicted that Prince Cor would one day save Archenland from the greatest danger it would ever have to face. How did Shasta make that prediction come true?

15. Azrooh was a Calormene lord who fought at the battle for Anvard. Who killed him?

16. After Rabadash's defeat what animal did Aslan turn him into? And how did he become a Human again?

17. Years later, Rabadash became Tisroc and would never leave Tashbaan to go to war with other countries. Why was this?

71

18. When did Bree become wiser?

19. Who begged his father to box Rabadash?

20. Even when they had grown up and settled in Archenland, Aravis and Shasta continued to argue before making up again. Why did they get married?

Reepicheep

1. Reepicheep was the Chief Mouse of all the Talking Mice in Narnia. However, the Mice of Narnia hadn't always been able to talk. When and why did they first become Talking Mice?

2. Why did Reepicheep sign on board the *Dawn Treader*?

3. Which crew member did Reepicheep think was a coward?

4. How did Reepicheep discover that the *Dawn Treader* was approaching Aslan's country?

5. While Eustace was a Dragon, how did Reepicheep comfort him?

6. According to the song the dryad sang to him when he was a young Mouse, where would Reepicheep find all he was looking for?

7. Who was Peepiceek?

8. What affectionate name did Caspian and the children on board the *Dawn Treader* sometimes call Reepicheep?

9. Who made Reepicheep a Knight of the Order of the Lion?

10. What kind of vessel did Reepicheep use on his final journey to Aslan's country?

11. Name the slave-trader who wanted to sell Reepicheep into slavery.

12. Who did Reepicheep challenge to a duel on board the *Dawn Treader*?

13. Even though he was a great and brave fighter, Reepicheep was not very good at playing chess, even with Lucy. Why?

14. What was the thing Lucy most wanted to do to Reepicheep, but never did, because she knew it would upset and embarrass him so much?

15. Who described Reepicheep as a vulgar performing animal?

16. In which battle had Reepicheep won undying glory?

17. What did Reepicheep wear upon his head?

18. Why did all the Talking Mice of Narnia offer to cut off their own tails?

19. When did Reepicheep finally throw away his sword?

20. After Lucy and Edmund said goodbye to Reepicheep at the end of *The Voyage of the Dawn Treader*, when did they next meet him?

The Magician's Nephew / 4

1. How were the animals of Narnia created?

2. After the animals of Narnia had been created, Aslan went among them, touching the noses of some animals and not some others. What happened to the animals that he touched with his nose?

3. What was the Neevil, or Weevil, which had entered Narnia before it was even five hours old?

4. How and why did Strawberry become a winged horse?

5. What was the First Joke?

6. What did the Talking Beasts of Narnia mistake for a Neevil, a tree, an animal, or even the Third Joke?

7. Of all the Humans, Digory was the most keen to talk to Aslan. What favour did he want to ask of Aslan?

8. And what was Aslan's response?

9. In the first few hours of Narnia who did a Rabbit mistake for a kind of large, talking lettuce?

10. Because he said this particular word so often, the Talking Beasts of Narnia supposed that it was Uncle Andrew's name. What was this word?

11. Who became the first King and Queen of Narnia?

12. For their journey into the Western Wild Digory and Polly had taken nothing to eat but nine lumps of toffee. They ate four lumps each. What did they do with the ninth piece of toffee?

13. How did Jadis try and tempt Digory in the orchard Aslan had sent him to?

14. What did the Tree of Protection protect Narnia from?

15. Who plucked an apple from the Tree of Protection?

16. Which creatures made the golden crowns which were used in the coronation of the first King and Queen of Narnia?

17. And where had the gold which they used for making these crowns come from?

18. How did Digory's mother get better again?

19. After Aslan had returned them all to their own world, what did Digory and Polly do to the magic rings?

20. Digory buried the core of the Apple he had brought back from Narnia in his back garden, and it grew into an apple tree. Years later, when Digory was grown up, the tree was blown over in a great storm. What did Digory then do to the tree?

The Last Battle / 4

1. He was the seventh son of Harpa Tarkaan of the city of Tehishbaan and had come to Narnia disguised as a merchant. What was his name?

2. How did Rishda Tarkaan meet his end?

3. Who brought Peter, Edmund, Lucy, Polly and Digory back to Narnia?

4. Who banished Tash back to his own place in the name of Aslan and of his father, the Emperor-over-the-Sea?

5. After the Last Battle for Narnia what was the first thing that Aslan told Peter, Eustace and Tirian to do?

6. Which Queen was more interested in nylons and lipsticks and never returned to Narnia when her brothers and sister did for the last time?

7. Calormenes often described other people as dogs. What do the Dogs of Narnia call their puppies when they don't behave properly?

8. Who was the opposite of Aslan?

9. How could Emeth come to Aslan's country, when he had been in the service of Tash all his life?

10. In the last days of Narnia Aslan called upon a Giant who lived near the banks of the River Shribble to blow his horn and call down all the stars from the sky. Jill and Eustace had seen the Giant once before. Who was he?

11. As night fell on Narnia, all living creatures came to Aslan, who was waiting for them by the Stable door. Those creatures who loved Aslan passed by him on his right side and headed off to Aslan's country. What happened to those creatures who hated Aslan?

12. After everyone had passed through Aslan's door, night finally fell on Narnia. What terrible creatures then took over Narnia and laid the country to waste, before they died and shrivelled away themselves?

13. Who did Aslan ask to destroy the sun of Narnia?

14. Which of the great heroes of Narnia welcomed Jill and Eustace and all the others to Aslan's country in Aslan's name?

15. When they had passed through the Stable door, who did the Talking Dogs find sitting under a chestnut tree by a stream?

16. Why did the Narnia that the children discovered behind the Stable door look more alive than the Narnia they had just seen destroyed?

17. Lucy met her dearest and oldest friend when she passed through the Stable door. Who was he?

18. Whose house, which Edmund thought had been destroyed, did they all see again when they passed through the Stable door?

19. What did Aslan call the Shadowlands?

20. What did Lucy finally realize was bigger inside than outside?

General / 8

1. What was the Great War of Deliverance?

2. Where was the Last Battle fought?
    (a) Beruna
    (b) Cair Paravel
    (c) Beaversdam
    (d) Lantern Waste

3. Although they never met each other, during the reign of King Miraz, Miss Prizzle and Doctor Cornelius shared the same sort of job. What was it?

4. Who did the Hags and the Dwarfs and similar people sometimes call the White Lady?

5   Where was Overworld?

6. Who was the magician who repaired the stern of the *Dawn Treader*, which had been damaged by the sea serpent?

7. Who didn't believe in Lions until he was thrown up in the air by one?

8. According to Eustace what is the only way one can get into Narnia?

9. Can you name one of the three Red Dwarfs who made Shasta breakfast when he arrived in Narnia?

10. Who is the only person who calls all times 'soon'?

11. Who or what were:
    (a) The Seven Brothers of Shuddering Wood
    (b) The Seven Lords
    (c) The Seven Isles

12. In which books do the following chapters appear?
    (a) What Lucy Saw
    (b) What Lucy Found There
    (c) What Caspian Did There
    (d) Jill Is Given a Task
    (e) Strawberry's Adventure
    (f) Shasta Falls in with the Narnians
    (g) How Help Came to the King

13. And in the chapters above:
    (a) What did Lucy see?
    (a) What did Lucy find there?
    (c) What did Caspian do there?

   (d) What was the task that Jill was given?

   (e) What was Strawberry's adventure?

   (f) Who were the Narnians Shasta fell in with?

   (g) What help came to the King?

14. Which of the Friends of Narnia, when he was an old man, wished that they would teach children Logic at school?

15. What did Aslan tell Peter, Susan, Edmund and Lucy to bear well?

16. Who were taken to the market on Doorn to be sold as slaves?

17. Who did Uncle Andrew always remember as a particularly fine woman?

18. According to Edmund who was an ass on his first visit to Narnia?

19. Why was Trumpkin very disappointed when he met Peter, Edmund, Susan and Lucy for the first time?

20. Which of the following is not a mountain?
   (a) Stormess
   (b) Lagour
   (c) Pire
   (d) Harfang

The Lion, the Witch and the Wardrobe / 5

1. What is written in spear-deep letters on the fire-stones of the Secret Hill?

2. How did the White Witch and the Dwarf escape from the rescue party that was sent to save Edmund?

3. Apart from the White Witch, who else in Narnia did the children meet who also drove a sleigh?

4. What would happen to Narnia if the White Witch was refused the blood that was hers according to the old laws?

5. When Aslan and the White Witch bargained for Edmund's life, what weapon did Aslan tell the Witch to leave behind?

6. Who offered up his own life for Edmund's?

7. What kind of animals carried Aslan's crown and standard when the children met him at the Stone Table?

8. Which of the children went with Aslan on his final journey to the Stone Table?

9. And who was waiting for Aslan at the Stone Table?

10. The White Witch knew all about the Deep Magic from the Dawn of Time. But who knew of a Deeper Magic from before the Dawn of Time?

11. And what was the Deeper Magic from before the Dawn of Time?

12. Apart from the White Witch and her people, who else was present when Aslan was killed?

13. What did the White Witch plan to do after she had killed Aslan?

14. After he had been killed, what kind of creatures gnawed away at the ropes with which the White Witch had tied up Aslan?

15. And who removed his muzzle?

16. Why did the Stone Table crack and split into two?

17. When they first saw him again after the Stone Table had split into two what did Lucy and Susan think Aslan was?

18. Lucy could never quite make up her mind whether it was like playing with a thunderstorm or a kitten. What was it?

19. After the breaking of the Stone Table where did Aslan take Susan and Lucy?

20. When was Edmund made a knight by Aslan?

The Land of Calormen

1. Calormen was a country that lay far to the south of the land of Narnia. What was the name of the country that could be found between Narnia and Calormen?

2. Who was the main god of the Calormene people?

3. Which King of Narnia, along with two children from our world, once disguised himself as a Calormene soldier?

4. What was the title of the powerful ruler of the Calormene people?

5. Which great Calormene city, known as one of the wonders of the world, was built on an island?

6. What was the Bight of Calormen?

7. Which Tarkaan did Ginger the Cat join forces with during the last days of Narnia?

8. Who were Azaroth and Zardeenah?

9. What kind of people did the Calormenes usually send to the salt-pits of Pugrahan?

10. What is a minim?

11. Which famous Talking Horse fought bravely with the Calormene army at the great Battle of Zelindrah?

12. Which of these is the odd one out: (a) Rabadash; (b) Aravis; (c) Gwendolen; and (d) Emeth?

13. What Calormene custom did Bree describe as fools' and slaves' talk?

14. Which leader of Calormen was known as the Peacemaker to his face, and as the Ridiculous behind his back?

15. Which King and Queen of Narnia visited Tashbaan with Prince Corin of Archenland?

16. Whose father was the Lord of Calavar province?

17. With what weapon was a Calormene soldier usually armed?

18. What sort of valley could you expect to find in Mezreel?

19. If a Calormene soldier called you his 'father', who would you be?

20. In the last days of Narnia, how did the men of Calormen attack Cair Paravel?

Out and About in Narnia and Beyond

1. What is the name of the country that lies between the lamp-post in the west and the great castle of Cair Paravel to the east?

2. Where would you find:
   (a) the Sunless Sea
   (b) the Silver Sea
   (c) the Pale Beaches?

3. Who lived in the east of Narnia, between two hills?

4. Where was Terebinthia?

5. Who lived ten miles from the nearest railway station and two miles from the nearest post office?

6. Where could you find the hunting lodge where King Tirian would often pass his time during the Last Days of Narnia?

7. Who lived in the Shuddering Wood?

8. Which Narnian river joins the Great River at the Bridge of Beruna?

9. What manner of creatures are usually to be found living on the banks of the River Shribble?

10. To which country would you have to go to see talkative Salamanders living in the fire?

11. Where was Burnt Island?

12. King Miraz's castle was built on the banks of Narnia's Great River. What lay directly opposite the castle of Caspian's wicked Uncle?

13. The old box that Uncle Andrew took from his old godmother when she died contained magic dust that had originally come from the Wood between the Worlds. But which magic land did the box itself come from?

14. Where in Narnia would you find the Great Waterfall?

15. On which of the Lone Islands would you find the town Bernstead?

16. For almost the whole of the history of Narnia, the Lone Islands were part of the royal lands of Narnia. How had they become part of Narnia?

17. In which country would you find Zelindrah and Tehishbaan?

18. Not all magicians come from places like Narnia. Which magician came from a very distinguished family in Dorsetshire?

19. Which one of the Ancient Places of Narnia was built on the site of the old Stone Table?

20. There was one main geographical difference between our world and the world of Narnia that made Caspian so keen to visit it. What was it?

General / 9

1. Where would you find the city of Azim Balda?
   (a) In Calormen
   (b) In Narnia
   (c) In Archenland
   (d) In Telmar

2. Where did Lucy discover a cure for warts?

3. Who were Voltinus, Dumnus, Obentinus and Nimienus?

4. In Narnia, what were the Ship, the Hammer and the Leopard?

5. Mrs Beaver was a very good seamstress and was given a sewing-machine by Father Christmas. Who else was very good with a needle and thread and even made a lion-suit for Puzzle the donkey to wear?

6. Which two Kings of Narnia separately fought the Northern Giants?

7. Slinky and Wraggle fought on the side of the Calormenes during the Last Battle. What kind of creatures were each of them?

8. Which animal can grant you all your wishes if you catch it?
   (a) A white Rabbit
   (b) A white Horse
   (c) A white Bear
   (d) A white Stag

9. Who was interested in reading about the habits of Nymphs and even had a book on his shelf about the subject?

10. Which animal had hearing so good that he could hear people whispering at Cair Paravel while he was sitting underneath the waterfall near Caldron Pool?

11. The sword of the High King Peter was called:
    (a) Rhindon
    (b) Rynelf
    (c) Rishda
    (d) Rogin

12. Where would you expect to find Cholmondley Major?

13. According to the old stories, who turned the giant Pire to stone?

14. Which of the following is the odd one out?
    (a) Lucy Pevensie
    (b) Eustace Scrubb
    (c) Adela Pennyfeather
    (d) Edith Jackle

15. Who welcomed the Friends of Narnia to Aslan's country in the Lion's name?

16. Who were vegetarians, non-smokers, wore a special kind of underwear and always kept the windows open?

17. Who of the following is a Calormene lord?
    (a) Corradin
    (b) Corin
    (c) Cor
    (d) Cornelius

18. After night had descended on Narnia who did Aslan tell to lock the door on the dead world?

19. According to Aslan in *The Voyage of the Dawn Treader*, what was the reason he had brought Lucy and Edmund into Narnia?

20. How did the Seven Friends of Narnia return to Narnia for the very last time in *The Last Battle*?

The Lion, the Witch and the Wardrobe / 6

1. Apart, of course, from Aslan, which person in *The Lion, the Witch and the Wardrobe* was present at the very beginning of Narnia?

2. What did Aslan, Susan and Lucy go searching for in the Witch's house?

3. Susan and Lucy were Daughters of Eve, because they were descended from Eve. Why might you be able to say that the White Witch was a Daughter of Lilith?

4. How did Aslan turn the statues in the Witch's house back into real living creatures again?

5. Who took Lucy and Susan to the Witch's house?

6. What was the name of the friendly Giant who helped Aslan and broke the gate of the Witch's house and freed all the ex-statues?

7. And what did Lucy lend him to wipe away his sweat after his hard work?

8. Who broke the White Witch's wand?

9. What was to be found on the front of Peter's shield?

10. In the final battle with the White Witch, Peter's army was outmanned. Who came to his help?

11. Who killed the White Witch?

12. Which of the Pevensie children looked after the wounded after the final battle with the White Witch and her army?

13. Why did Aslan choose Peter to be High King over all the others?

14. Where did Aslan crown Peter, Susan, Edmund and Lucy as Kings and Queens of Narnia?

15. When they became Kings and Queens, which of the children were known as:
    (a) The Gentle
    (b) The Magnificent
    (c) The Valiant
    (d) The Just?

16. Who brought news of the reappearance of the White Stag to Kings Peter and Edmund and Queens Susan and Lucy?

17. Towards the end of the children's reign as Kings and Queens of Narnia the White Stag had been spotted again. Where had it been seen?

18. Where did the White Stag lead Kings Peter and Edmund, and Queens Susan and Lucy?

19. Ivy, Margaret and Betty didn't play a big part in this story. Who were they?

20. How did Professor Kirke tell the children they would know if other people had been to Narnia?

The Life and Works of C.S. Lewis

1. What do the initials in C.S. Lewis's name stand for?

2. And what was his nickname to his friends and family?

3. Although he lived for most of his life in England where was Lewis born?

4. Lewis said that he first saw the Chronicles of Narnia as a series of pictures in his head and that then it was his job to put the pictures together into some kind of story. Who was the very first character he saw in his imagination when he was only sixteen years old?

5. At which two great and famous English universities did Lewis teach English Language and Literature?

6. Which of Lewis's friends also created another imaginary world, which was populated with heroes and dragons, magicians and demons?

7. Long before he wrote the Chronicles of Narnia, Lewis wrote about another magical land where all the animals could talk. What was that land called?

8. According to Lewis this character wasn't going to feature in the Narnia books at all, until he appeared to him in a dream. Who was this character?

9. One of Lewis's books is called *The Screwtape Letters*. Who is Screwtape, and what is the book about?

10. In 1957, which of the Chronicles of Narnia won the Carnegie Medal, the top prize for children's fiction in Great Britain?

11. Between 1938 and 1945 Lewis wrote a series of science-fiction books called the *Space Trilogy* and telling of the adventures of a man called Ransom. Can you name one of these books?

12. What was the name of the television play and movie written about Lewis and which told of his love for the American Joy Gresham, who was dying of cancer?

13. Who did Lewis base the character of Puddleglum on?

14. Which artist drew the illustrations for the original Chronicles of Narnia?

15. Who were the Inklings?

16. During the Second World War, when the bombs were falling on London, Lewis did something, which Professor Kirke would later do in *The Lion, the Witch and the Wardrobe*. What did he do?

17. Which characters did Lewis originally call Peter, Ann, Martin and Rose?

18. Which of Lewis's friends disliked *The Lion, the Witch and the Wardrobe* so much that Lewis almost didn't finish writing the book?

19. Which of the Chronicles of Narnia did Lewis think about calling *The Wild Waste Lands*?

20. Lewis was born in 1898. When did he die?

The Answers

General / 1 – page 3

1. Aslan.

2. Peter (who became High King), Susan, Edmund and Lucy.

3. Digory. He knew so much about Narnia, because he had already been there (in *The Magician's Nephew*).

4. (b) A Faun (Mr Tumnus).

5. Because time in Narnia flows differently than in our world.

6. In the house of the White Witch.

7. (a) Rilian; (b) Caspian; (c) Corin

8. (b) Moles.

9. It was made from the wood of a tree that had grown from the core of an apple Digory had brought back from Narnia.

10. Cair Paravel.

11. (a) Caspian (he was also known as the Seafarer).

12. (b) She used a magic wand.

13. *The Lion, the Witch and the Wardrobe* (1950); *Prince Caspian* (1952); *The Voyage of the Dawn Treader* (1952); *The Silver Chair* (1953); *The Horse and His Boy* (1954); *The Magician's Nephew* (1955); *The Last Battle* (1956).

14. *The Magician's Nephew*; *The Lion, the Witch and the Wardrobe*; *The Horse and His Boy*; *Prince Caspian*; *The Voyage of the Dawn Treader*; *The Silver Chair*; *The Last Battle*.

15. On the side of the White Witch.

16. The Talking Beasts, and the Dwarfs and all those other creatures who were in hiding during the reign of the evil King Miraz.

17. The Telmarines who ruled Narnia at that time.

18. (a) Aslan.

19. You will find a way into Narnia.

20. (a) Deathwater is an island in the Great Eastern Ocean; (b) Goldwater is another name for Deathwater; (c) Glasswater is a tiny bay off the coast of Narnia, a few miles south of Cair Paravel.

The Lion, the Witch and the Wardrobe / 1 – page 5

1. Like many other children at the time, they were sent to the country to escape the bombs that were falling on London during the Second World War.

2. A dead bluebottle on the window-ledge.

3. Mr Tumnus, the faun.

4. She was Professor Kirke's housekeeper, who didn't like children.

5. The White Witch.

6. Professor Kirke.

7. Lucy, or so Mr Tumnus thought. (He had misheard Lucy when she had told him she had come from the wardrobe in the spare room.)

8. Because she knew that it was a very stupid thing to do shut yourself up in a wardrobe.

9. Peter was the oldest, followed by Susan, Edmund and finally Lucy, the youngest.

10. Edmund.

11. Sorrow.

12. Snow.

13. The White Witch.

14. A lamp-post.

15. Mr Tumnus.

16. All the Turkish Delight he could eat.

17. Mr and Mrs Beaver and Peter, Susan and Lucy.

18. Susan and Lucy were the Daughters of Eve, and the Sons of Adam were Peter and Edmund.

19. It was raining too hard for them to be able to go and play outside.

20. Edmund.

Prince Caspian / 1 – page 7

1. Prince Caspian when he blew Susan's magic horn, which would always bring help to Narnia when it was blown.

2. At a railway station, waiting for the trains to take them back to school.

3. Lucy.

4. Miraz.

5. Trumpkin. The D.L.F. stood for Dear Little Friend and was the nickname the children gave him.

6. Because it was said that Aslan always came to Narnia from over the sea.

7. Caspian's uncle, Miraz.

8. His old nurse.

9. She was sent away from King Miraz when he learnt that she had been telling Caspian stories of Old Narnia.

10. The ruins of Cair Paravel, the castle in which they had ruled as Kings and Queens hundreds of years ago in Narnia.

11. He and his fellow Telmarines conquered Narnia.

12. A rainbow-coloured fish which Peter, Susan, Edmund and Lucy used to eat when they were Kings and Queens of Narnia, and which Trumpkin caught for them after they had saved his life.

13. The Old Narnians, who lived in hiding from King Miraz and the Telmarines.

14. Prince Caspian.

15. They were told the story by Trumpkin.

16. Lucy.

17. They believed ghosts lived there.

18. The wife of King Miraz and Caspian's aunt.

19. A Mole who helped plant the orchard at Cair Paravel.

20. Wimbleweather.

The Voyage of the Dawn Treader / 1 – page 8

1. He was drawn into Narnia by the magic painting of the *Dawn Treader* that was hanging on the wall of Lucy's bedroom when she was staying with Eustace over the summer holidays.

2. A Dragon.

3. He wanted to bully them.

4. Susan was in America with their parents and Peter was staying in the country with old Professor Kirke to study for an important exam.

5. Three years.

6. Caspian.

7. Eustace had grabbed the Mouse's tail and spun him around in the air on the deck of the *Dawn Treader*.

8. Drinian.

9. He was sailing off to find the seven Lords who his wicked Uncle Miraz had sent into exile after Miraz had murdered Caspian's father.

10. In Caspian's cabin, which Caspian had given up for her.

11. A mate on board the *Dawn Treader*.

12. Eustace.

13. Purple.

14. Eustace.

15. The Seven Isles.

16. The Lone Islands.

17. Gumpas.

18. The Lone Islands were Doorn, Felimath and Avra.

19. Governor Gumpas of the Lone Islands.

20. Eustace Clarence Scrubb.

Aslan / 1 – page 10

1. A Lion.

2. Lucy.

3. Susan.

4. Eustace (when he was a Dragon).

5. Children from our world.

6. Nine.

7. A cat.

8. He playfully threw him up in the air.

9. The east.

10. The appearance of Father Christmas in Narnia, and the White Witch's winter ending and spring returning to Narnia.

11. Puzzle, the donkey.

12. Father Time.

13. Emeth.

14. Lucy and Susan.

15. He offered up his own life for Edmund's.

16. Peter, Susan, Edmund and Lucy.

17. (a) *The Voyage of the Dawn Treader;* (b) *The Horse and His Boy*; (c). *The Voyage of the Dawn Treader.*

18. In *The Silver Chair* when he took Eustace, Jill and Caspian back to Experiment House.

19. It was a mound in the north of Narnia, which had been built on the site of the old Stone Table.

20. The White Witch.

General / 2 – page 11

1. Digory, Polly, Peter, Edmund, Lucy, Eustace and Jill.

2. Aslan.

3. Mr Tumnus.

4. Mrs Beaver.

5. He had been greedy and had eaten too much of the White Witch's enchanted Turkish Delight.

6. *Prince Caspian*.

7. An aristocratic lady from Calormen. Aravis was a Tarkheena.

8. (a) *The Silver Chair*; (b) *The Horse and His Boy*; (c) *The Last Battle*; (d) *The Lion, the Witch and the Wardrobe*; (e) *The Voyage of the Dawn Treader*; (f) *The Magician's Nephew*; (g) *Prince Caspian*.

9. (b) A hundred years.

10. Dwarfs.

11. They were all the same person.

12. A dryad is a spirit of the trees.

13. A naiad is a spirit of the rivers and wells.

14. Cair Paravel.

15. Jadis, the Cabby, Uncle Andrew and Strawberry, the Horse, Later, Aslan brought from our world into Narnia Nellie, the cabby's wife, who was to become Queen Helen, the very first Queen of Narnia.

16. (a) The *Dawn Treader* was Caspian's ship; (b) The *Splendour Hyaline* was the ship of Kings Peter and Edmund, and Queens Susan and Lucy.

17. (a) King Tirian; (b) King Caspian the Tenth (Prince Caspian); (c) King Cor (Shasta).

18. Edmund.

19. Edmund (in *The Lion, the Witch and the Wardrobe*) and Susan (in *The Last Battle*).

20. Jadis, the White Witch.

The Silver Chair / 1 – page 13

1. Jill and Eustace. Pole and Scrubb were their last names. (At their school people never called each other by their first names.)

2. Experiment House.

3. He had travelled to Narnia, with his cousins, Lucy and Edmund, and had become a nicer and kinder boy.

4. They called on Aslan to take them there.

5. They arrived on the top of a high cliff of one of the mountains that circle the world in which Narnia is to be found.

6. Aslan. Jill was worried that Aslan might attack her, and was about to look for another stream when Aslan told her that there was none.

7. Aslan. He blew them there with his breath.

8. He had fallen off the cliff edge while he was trying to stop Jill from going too close to the edge.

9. Trumpkin.

10. Aslan told them that they had to go and search for the disappeared Prince Rilian, until they had found him and brought him back to his father, King Caspian, or died trying, or returned to their own world.

11. The first sign was that the very first person Eustace met in Narnia would be an old friend that he should greet if they wanted good luck in their quest. The second sign was that Eustace and Jill had to journey north to the ruined city of the ancient Giants. The third sign was that they had to do what the writing on a stone in that ruined city told them to do. And the fourth and final sign was that the lost prince Rilian would be the very first person they would meet who would ask them to do something in the name of Aslan.

12. Prince Rilian.

13. His father was King Caspian the Tenth and his mother was Ramandu's daughter, who Caspian had first met during the voyage of the *Dawn Treader*.

14. A great green serpent who was really the Lady of the Green Kirtle, the Queen of Underland who enchanted Prince Rilian.

15. King Caspian, who Eustace had known as Prince Caspian when he sailed with him to the eastern edge of the world during the voyage of the *Dawn Treader*. He didn't recognize him because seventy years had passed in Narnia and Caspian was now a very old man.

16. Because they had missed the first of the four signs which Aslan had given to them.

17. Puddleglum, the Marsh-wiggle.

18. Because he had heard a rumour that Aslan had been seen (possibly on the island of Terebinthia) and he wanted to see Aslan and ask him who should be King of Narnia after him. However, some Narnians were afraid that if Caspian didn't find Aslan there then he would travel on to the very end of the world and never come back.

19. The River Shribble.

20. Giants.

The Horse and His Boy / 1 – page 14

1. Shasta.

2. Bree.

3. Hwin.

4. Arsheesh.

5. He was found by Arsheesh as a baby in a small boat floating down the river, and was adopted by the fisherman as his own son – although 'slave' might be the more proper word.

6. Aravis. (Aravis was the daughter of Kidrash Tarkaan, who was the son of Rishti Tarkaan, who was the son of Kidrash, who was the son of Ilsombreh, who was the son of Ardeeb Tisroc.)

7. Because he had always felt guilty about never really having loved Arsheesh as a father.

8. Because he overheard Arsheesh discussing selling him into slavery with the Tarkaan.

9. He had been captured by Humans when he was just a foal and had been wandering the southern slopes into Archenland and beyond (against his mother's advice).

10. Alimash was Aravis's cousin.

11. They would have a much better chance of escape together, and, with a rider on his back, Bree would never be mistaken for a stray horse.

12. Tashbaan in the north. From there they planned to travel onwards to Narnia.

13. Queen Susan.

14. Holding on with the knees, sitting up straight, and keeping the elbows tucked in.

15. They met weeks after Shasta had escaped. They were both crossing a wide plain in the dark, when they were both set upon and chased by a pack of lions. (Later they discovered that the 'lions' were, in fact, Aslan.)

16. She wanted to escape being married to Ahoshta Tarkaan, an ugly sixty-year-old man with a hump on his back and a face like an ape's.

17. It was the only way she could think of to avoid being married to Ahoshta.

18. Hwin. She told her that in Narnia she would be free and could marry whoever she wanted.

19. She drugged one of her serving-maids, and left her father's house, disguised in the armour of her dead brother. So that her father wouldn't follow her, she then forged a letter from the man she was to marry telling father they had already got married.

20. Narnia.

The Magician's Nephew / 1 – page 15

1. Digory's Uncle Andrew, Mr Ketterley.

2. Digory.

3. Polly.

4. Jadis, the last Queen of Charn. In *The Lion, the Witch and the Wardrobe* she was better known as the White Witch.

5. His father was in India, and his mother, who was going to die, needed to be looked after.

6. In the secret tunnel that ran behind all the houses in the terrace where she and Digory lived.

7. He was crying because he had moved from the country to London, but mainly because his mother was going to die.

8. Uncle Andrew's study.

9. Kirke.

10. Uncle Andrew.

11. He realized that he could use them in his experiments with the magic rings. (He had already experimented on a guinea-pig.)

12. Green and yellow.

13. Dust that had been brought to our world from the Wood between the Worlds.

14. He offered her one of the yellow rings as a present. The moment she touched it she vanished from our world.

15. He told Digory that Polly could only return to our world if she had a green ring, and that Digory had to take one to her.

16. He told Digory to remember G for Green and R for Right: G and R are the first letters of the word 'green'.

17. An in-between place, filled with pools that would take you to all sorts of different worlds (if you were wearing the right kind of magic ring, of course).

18. A guinea-pig. Uncle Andrew had sent it there on one of his first experiments with the magic rings.

19. The yellow rings took anyone wearing them *into* the Wood between the Worlds. The green rings took anyone wearing them *out of* the Wood between the Worlds.

20. Charn.

The Last Battle / 1 – page 17

1. In a tree-house near the Great Waterfall in the west of Narnia beyond Lantern Waste.

2. Puzzle. He was a Donkey.

3. That Aslan had been seen in Narnia again.

4. The birds.

5. The High King Peter, King Edmund, Queen Lucy, Lord Digory, Lady Polly, Jill and Eustace.

6. The skin of a dead lion.

7. He thought they should bury it.

8. Calormen, in the south.

9. He told them he was a very wise Man, hundreds of years old.

10. Jewel.

11. A wise and noble Centaur.

12. Because he had not read of it in the stars. In fact, he had never known of a more ill-omened set of signs in the stars for the last five centuries, and he feared that something dreadful was about to happen to Narnia.

13. He was warned by a dryad, the spirit of a Talking Tree that was even then being cut down in Lantern Waste.

14. Puzzle, under the orders of Shift the Ape who was working with Rishda Tarkaan.

15. Aslan.

16. For fun, and also because he had a feeling that they were needed in Narnia.

17. Shift the Ape.

18. Aslan, and then the Friends of Narnia (Peter, Edmund, Lucy, Digory, Polly, Jill and Eustace).

19. Shift, after Shift had claimed that Aslan and Tash were one and the same person.

20. Puzzle.

General / 3 – page 18

1. Susan.

2. Charn.

3. (c) The Wood between the Worlds.

4. (c) Puddleglum.

5. (a) Jill first met Aslan in *The Silver Chair*; (b) Eustace first met Caspian in *The Voyage of the Dawn Treader*; (c) Polly (and Digory) first met Aslan in *The Magician's Nephew*.

6. (d) Puddleglum. Puddleglum is a Marsh-wiggle. All the others are Giants.

7. The Giant Porter in Harfang.

8. Edmund, Lucy and Eustace.

9. (a) A Hare.

10. Mr Tumnus.

11. The White Witch.

12. Aslan.

13. (b) Turkish Delight.

14. (c) His tail.

15. Mabel.

16. (c) An apple.

17. *The Horse and His Boy*.

18. They are both former stars.

19. Susan.

20. The autumn.

The Kings and Queens of Narnia – page 20

1. King Tirian.

2. Aslan.

3. King Caspian the Tenth (Prince Caspian).

4. (c) Aravis. Aravis became Queen of Archenland.

5. Kings Peter and Edmund, and Queens Susan and Lucy.

6. Peter.

7. King Caspian the Tenth (Prince Caspian).

8. Cair Paravel.

9. Rilian.

10. Queen Helen.

11. Swanwhite.

12. The Cabby, who became King Frank, the very first King of Narnia in *The Magician's Nephew*.

13. He was also called Caspian.

14. Rilian.

15. King Edmund. He was also the Count of the Western March and a Knight of the Noble Order of the Table.

16. The *Splendour Hyaline*.

17. She claimed to be descended from Adam's first wife, Lilith. (In truth, Lilith was a Jinn and so the White Witch had no real claim to be Queen of Narnia.)

18. Ramandu's daughter.

19. She was killed by a green serpent that was, in reality, the Queen of the Underland.

20. Queen Lucy.

The Lion, the Witch and the Wardrobe / 2 – page 21

1. Mr Tumnus.

2. She turned them into stone statues.

3. Because when they looked inside the Wardrobe they discovered that it was just a normal everyday wardrobe, and there was nothing magical about it.

4. Make some proper roads.

5. A Dwarf.

6. She wanted to have one more look inside to prove to herself that it hadn't been a dream.

7. He followed her in there to make fun of her.

8. A Wolf and the Chief of the Witch's Secret Police.

9. A hundred years.

10. It was magic and, no matter how much of it anyone ate, they would always want more.

11. Geography.

12. Because he didn't know where the city of War Drobe or the land of Spare Oom were.

13. He wanted to spite Lucy.

14. She told him that if he ever saw a Son of Adam or a Daughter of Eve, he was to kidnap them and bring them to her.

15. Edmund.

16. To bring Peter and Susan and Lucy to her.

17. He said that because Lucy never lied, and because she didn't appear to be mad, then it was very likely that she was telling the truth about Narnia.

18. They went in there to hide from Mrs Macready who was showing visitors around the house.

19. Mr Tumnus.

20. They wore the fur coats that they had found hanging in the wardrobe.

Prince Caspian / 2 – page 23

1. Over a thousand years.

2. One year.

3. King Miraz, his uncle.

4. Because his wife gave birth to a son, who he wanted be King after him. As Caspian was the rightful King of Narnia he had to be killed.

5. The Great River of Narnia.

6. Susan.

7. She had lost it on the day they had gone out to hunt the White Stag (in *The Lion, the Witch and the Wardrobe*). Many hundreds of years later, it had been found by Doctor Cornelius and he had given it to Prince Caspian.

8. Red.

9. Telmar.

10. Prince Caspian's ancestors had all come from Telmar.

11. His old nurse.

12. The star Alambil, which Prince Caspian and Doctor Cornelius viewed from one of the towers of King Miraz's castle.

13. Aslan (although at first they were pursued by a bear).

14. He was a half-dwarf.

15. After Caspian had fallen off his horse, Destrier, it had returned to King Miraz's Castle.

16. A Mole and one of the Old Narnians who befriended Prince Caspian.

17. He was a Centaur. He and his three sons joined Prince Caspian and the other Old Narnians.

18. Trumpkin.

19. Aslan.

20. Aslan brought her to him after the Telmarines had been defeated.

The Voyage of the Dawn Treader / 2 – page 24

1. The men of Calormen.

2. The Lone Islands. A Calormene crescent is worth about one third of a pound.

3. The Isle of Wight.

4. With the magic cordial that Father Christmas had given her when she had first come to Narnia, and which Caspian had brought with him on board the *Dawn Treader*.

5. Beetles (as long as they were dead and pinned on pieces of card).

6. The seven Lords were: Argoz; Bern; Mavramorn; Octesian; Restimar; Revilian; and Rhoop.

7. Pug.

8. Reepicheep.

9. Eustace.

10. Eustace.

11. On the Lone Island of Doorn.

12. Caspian reminded him so much of his former master, King Caspian IX (Caspian's father). The man who bought Caspian was the Lord Bern, one of the seven Lords evil King Miraz had sent off into exile.

13. They pretended to send signals out to their other ships telling them to prepare for battle.

14. The Lord Bern.

15. He fell asleep on a Dragon's treasure hoard, and with selfish Dragon-like thoughts in his head he became a Dragon himself.

16. The Lord Octesian.

17. Eustace when he was stuck in the shape of a Dragon.

18. Reepicheep.

19. Aslan.

20. He ripped Eustace's Dragon skin off him.

The Talking Beasts of Narnia / 1 – page 26

1. Aslan made certain animals Talking Beasts when he created Narnia in *The Magician's Nephew*.

2. They were slightly larger.

3. Reepicheep.

4. A Stag.

5. A Wolf. Fenris Ulf was the name by which Maugrim, the chief of the White Witch's Secret Police, was known in some editions of *The Lion, the Witch and the Wardrobe*.

6. He knew that if anyone discovered he could speak he would be paraded as a circus attraction.

7. Strawberry, the Cabby's Horse.

8. A Fox.

9. She turned them all into stone statues.

10. A Parliament of Owls.

11. Reepicheep and Trufflehunter.

12. A Hare.

13. Peepiceek.

14. He ran out of the stable where he had seen Tash and was never seen again.

15. A Talking Stag.

16. A Lion.

17. A Unicorn.

18. Glimfeather, the Owl.

19. Reepicheep.

20. Aslan.

General / 4 – page 27

1. The North.

2. King Caspian. He was sailing off to try and see Aslan and ask him his advice about who should be King after him.

3. Aslan.

4. When they came to stay with him during the War. (Digory grew up to become old Professor Kirke.)

5. They thought that they were both on the same side with evil plots against Narnia.

6. He thought of calling *The Silver Chair Gnomes Under Narnia*, and *Narnia and the North* seemed like a good title for the book that was to become *The Horse and His Boy*.

7. (a) Ghosts.

8. (d) Gumpas. (Gumpas was the Governor of the Lone Islands. All the others are Dwarfs.)

9. Edmund.

10. Lucy and Edmund (according to Eustace at the beginning of *The Voyage of the Dawn Treader*).

11. Trumpkin.

12. King Frank; Queen Swanwhite; the White Witch; High King Peter; King Caspian IX; King Miraz; King Caspian the Tenth (Prince Caspian); King Tirian.

13. Reepicheep.

14. Coalblack – Prince Rilian; Destrier – Prince Caspian; Strawberry – Frank the Cabby; Bree – Shasta; Snowflake – the Queen of Underland.

15. Edmund.

16. (c) A shield.

17. Evil creatures who were in the service of the White Witch.

18. Archenland and Calormen.

19. Jill and Eustace.

20. Father Christmas returning to Narnia.

The Silver Chair / 2 – page 29

1. An Owl.

2. He lost his balance when he tried to stop Jill from standing too close to the edge of the cliff. (Jill admitted later to Aslan that she had been showing off.)

3. The four signs that he had given to her to help her and Eustace in their quest for Prince Rilian.

4. At Experiment House, Jill and Eustace's school.

5. The frog-like people who lived in the Marshes in the north of Narnia on the banks of the River Shribble. Puddleglum was a Marsh-wiggle.

6. He had met the Lady of the Green Kirtle (the Queen of Underland) and had fallen under her enchantment.

7. The lady called herself the Lady of the Green Kirtle but was really the Queen of Underland. The knight was the enchanted Prince Rilian.

8. A skeleton – or nothing at all, or someone invisible.

9. Jill, Eustace and Puddleglum (she knew that the Giants would eat them as part of the Autumn Feast).

10. Drinian asked Caspian to kill him as a traitor because he hadn't stopped Prince Rilian from going off with the Witch. Caspian was tempted to kill but decided that he didn't want to lose his friend, after having also lost his wife and his son.

11. Glimfeather and his fellow Owls.

12. If Trumpkin (who was in charge of Narnia while the King was away) learnt of their plan to look for the lost Prince, then he would have stopped them.

13. His fellow Marsh-wiggles.

14. They believed Prince Rilian was still alive because his bones had never been found.

15. Wigwams.

16. Eels.

17. Ten years.

18. Because they eat so much, as they have two stomachs to feed – a man-stomach and a horse-stomach.

19. Because Giants live there.
20. The Queen of Underland.

The Horse and His Boy / 2 – page 31

1. Tash.

2. The fisherman wanted to sell him for seventy crescents. The Tarkaan was prepared to offer fifteen crescents. (Shasta knew that after lots of arguing they would settle at a figure somewhere in between. However, he didn't stay to find out.)

3. Rolling in the grass.

4. Because Bree was a war horse and war horses are too expensive to be treated badly.

5. High King Peter.

6. The Tisroc, the leader of the Calormenes.

7. Bree. He told her that she could just as well say that he, Bree, had stolen Shasta.

8. Because they believed the tombs were haunted by ghosts.

9. King Edmund and Queen Susan.

10. Shasta and Aravis disguised themselves as peasants or slaves.

11. Bree and Hwin rolled around in the mud to look dirty and had their tails cut shorter (much to Bree's annoyance!).

12. Anradin was Bree's master and the Tarkaan who tried to buy Shasta as a slave from Arsheesh.

13. One of the Narnian Lords who travelled with King Edmund and Queen Susan to Tashbaan and led the defence against Prince Rabadash's army.

14. Lasareleen.

15. Because, as a Calormene, she was taught the art of storytelling (just as children in our world are taught how to write essays).

16. Because they thought he was Prince Corin, who had been missing all night.

17. A Hedgehog.

18. He was kidnapped by the traitor Lord Bar, who was in the pay of the Tisroc, who had heard a prediction that Cor would save Archenland from a deadly threat. King Lune (Cor's father) defeated Bar, but Cor was taken away by one of Bar's men who took Cor down the river (where Cor was found by Arsheesh).

19. Bree. (He was given the sugar by Aravis's cousin, Alimash.)

20. A cat (who was really Aslan).

The Magician's Nephew / 2 – page 33

1. The Wood between the Worlds.

2. They were three of the last people in the country to have fairy blood.

3. You would be taken to another world.

4. It was red and much larger than the sun in our world. Digory knew that it was nearing the end of its life.

5. Images of the ancestors of Jadis, and, of course, Jadis herself.

6. To strike the bell and to see what would happen. If they didn't they would go mad wondering what might have happened.

7. He wanted to see what would happen. (To be fair, he was very probably enchanted at that moment.)

8. Jadis awoke from her long enchanted sleep.

9. Jadis.

10. Charn, the city that Jadis had ruled over.

11. A word which, when spoken with certain rites, would destroy everything living, apart from the person who spoke the word.

12. Jadis. She spoke it when all her armies had been defeated by her sister's rebels.

13. Escape from the ruins of Charn and use Digory and Polly to take her to our world and then to conquer it.

14. Because he was a magician and in her world only people of royal blood were magicians.

15. They had all been destroyed by Jadis.

16. Uncle Andrew. He pawned his watch and chain so that he could take her out to a restaurant.

17. The Cabby's horse that was stolen by Jadis to drive her 'chariot' around London.

18. Fledge was the name the Cabby's horse was called by Aslan after Aslan had changed him into a winged horse.

19. Digory (although Polly didn't see anything beautiful about her at all).

20. Letitia ('Letty').

117

The Last Battle / 2 – page 35

1. A wily ginger Cat and one of Shift's allies who also made plans with Rishda Tarkaan.

2. Impersonate Aslan.

3. Tash, the god of the Calormene people.

4. Because Aslan had told the others that they were too old ever to return to Narnia.

5. They planned to use the magic rings that Digory and Polly had used to travel to Narnia when they were children (in *The Magician's Nephew*).

6. A tiny hut that looked like a stable.

7. Jill. (In our world Jill had also been an excellent Guide.)

8. The great waterfall poured into it, churning the water like the water in a cauldron, before it flowed into the Great River of Narnia.

9. A group of Talking Beasts – three Mice, two Moles and one Rabbit. (They didn't dare to untie him however, because they thought that 'Aslan' might be angry with them.)

10. One year.

11. They made their way to one of three towers that had been built to guard Lantern Waste against outlaws. Tirian still had the keys for these towers.

12. They disguised themselves as Calormene soldiers.

13. She knew that the hissing sound of the letter 's' is the part of a whisper that is the easiest to overhear.

14. Jill.

15. He claimed that Aslan had swallowed him up whole, which frightened the Narnians even more.

16. Roonwit the Centaur.

17. The Dwarfs.

18. Because no Talking Lions ever came that far west into the Western Wilds.

19. In Aslan's Country.

20. The name Shift invented for the false Aslan. Shift claimed that Aslan and Tash were, in fact, the same person.

General / 5 – page 37

1. The Marsh-wiggles.

2. (b) Two stars (their conjunction in *Prince Caspian* predicted great good fortune for the troubled land of Narnia).

3. (a) The house of the White Witch; (b) Professor Kirke's house; (c) the house of the 'gentle' Giants at Harfang.

4. Trees and Lions.

5. Prince Caspian and the Old Narnians.

6. (b) His torch.

7. (c) Earthmen. The Earthmen were the gnomes who worked for the Queen of Underland.

8. The beginning and the end of Narnia.

9. They had been fooled by a false Aslan before and refused to be fooled again.

10. It made him stronger.

11. (b) Prince Rilian would ask them to do something for him in Aslan's name.

12. Bacchus was the god of wine. We finally met him in *Prince Caspian*.

113. To Narnia. (The first entry in his diary was dated 7 August, and in there he says that he has been on board the *Dawn Treader* for twenty-four hours.)

14. (c) Harpa. He was a Calormene Lord and Emeth's father.

15. A stable in *The Last Battle*.

16. (d) Eustace.

17. The table on Ramandu's Island which was stocked with food every day and where the Lords Argoz, Mavramorn and Revilian slept in an enchanted sleep.

18. Aslan.

19. The Great Snow Dance.

20. (c) King Cor (Shasta) was a King of Archenland.

Of Witches, Wizards and Werewolves – page 39

1. Jadis from *The Magician's Nephew* and the White Witch from *The Lion, the Witch and the Wardrobe* were one and the same person.

2. She ate one of the Apples of Youth from the Orchard in Aslan's country.

3. The White Witch, according to Mr Beaver.

4. Coriakin (from *The Voyage of the Dawn Treader*).

5. Uncle Andrew.

6. The Deplorable Word. If anyone spoke the Deplorable Word, then all living things would die (apart from the person who spoke it).

7. With her magic wand.

8. It was taken to Ramandu's Island where it was preserved in honour until the world ends.

9. The White Witch.

10. Uncle Andrew's godmother was one of the three last people in England to have fairy blood in her veins. (The other two were a duchess and a charwoman.)

11. To burn the box from Atlantis which contained the dust out of which Uncle Andrew's magic rings were made. (Uncle Andrew ignored her request, of course.)

12. She played a mandolin and lit a magic fire, which placed them all under an enchantment until they no longer believed in Narnia, or even in Aslan.

13. The Werewolf, Nikabrik's friend in Aslan's How who wanted to bring the White Witch back to Narnia.

14. Nikabrik's.

15. Digory.

16. (b) The centaurs.

17. The White Witch when she was Queen of Narnia.

18. Prince Rilian.

19. Prince Caspian.

20. Jadis.

The Lion, the Witch and the Wardrobe / 3 – page 40

1. A slab of grey rock supported on four upright stones. It was very old and covered with strange inscriptions. It was here that the White Witch killed Aslan.

2. A sleigh, driven by reindeer.

3. He started giving directions to the lamp-post.

4. Professor Kirke.

5. Because he had been consorting with the enemy, when he should have kidnapped Lucy and taken her to the White Witch when he had the chance.

6. The White Witch had earlier told him never to trust Fauns.

7. Mr Tumnus and Mr Beaver.

8. She wanted him to bring his brother and sisters into Narnia.

9. A Beaver.

10. A Robin.

11. To Mr Beaver.

12. A handkerchief.

13. Mr and Mrs Beaver.

14. Because the whole of Narnia was inside the Wardrobe, she said that they couldn't be accused of taking them from the Wardrobe.

15. Mr and Mrs Beaver.

16. Edmund felt a feeling of horror.

17. Aslan.

18. He headed to the White Witch's house to tell her that he had brought Peter, Susan and Lucy into Narnia – and to get some more Turkish Delight.

19. Maugrim, the Wolf.

20. Aslan's name.

Prince Caspian / 3 – page 42

1. Trumpkin, Nikabrik and Trufflehunter.

2. Trumpkin and Nikabrik were Dwarfs and Trufflehunter was a Badger.

3. To King Nain of Archenland.

4. Because from there they couldn't be overheard.

5. That all the stories about Old Narnia were true.

6. At the Dancing Lawn.

7. Aslan's How; Cair Paravel to the east; and Lantern Waste to the west.

8. It is considered bad manners.

9. He challenged him to a duel.

10. Edmund.

11. Red Dwarfs who gave armour to Prince Caspian.

12. From an island in the South Seas from our own world.

13. She was a school-teacher at a girls' school near Beruna who fled with most of her pupils when Aslan destroyed the school she taught in.

14. A Hag and a Werewolf.

15. They wanted to bring back the White Witch.

16. Two Telmarine Lords who betrayed King Miraz.

17. A Black Dwarf.

18. Susan. She managed to hit a tiny red apple hanging from a tree branch that the Dwarf had missed.

19. His old nurse.

20. King Miraz.

The Voyage of the Dawn Treader / 3 – page 44

1. Being turned into a Dragon.

2. Eustace's parents.

3. Because the water in that island turned everything – and everyone – to gold.

4. Because the Lord Restimar died when he was turned to gold after he went for a swim in one of the island's pools; and because the island awakened great greed and evil in the hearts of men.

5. The Lord Restimar.

6. The Utter East and Aslan's Country.

7. Coriakin.

8. The Dufflepuds (they were also called Duffers and Monopods).

9. In the magic book of spells and enchantments which belonged to Coriakin.

10. Coriakin, when they disobeyed him.

11. They turned themselves invisible because they were so ashamed of how ugly they thought they looked.

12. Because the spells in the Magician's Book would only work if spoken by the Magician or a little girl.

13. Two of Lucy's school friends. She used the Magician's Book to eavesdrop on them, and was upset by what she heard.

14. Aslan and Coriakin, the Magician himself.

15. Coriakin.

16. Warts.

17. The Dufflepuds (or Monopods).

18. Nightmares also came true on that island.

19. Rhoop.

20. Aslan.

Aslan / 2 – page 46

1. The Emperor-over-the-Sea.

2. Reepicheep.

3. Lucy (even though the others didn't believe her at first).

4. Caspian (in *The Silver Chair*).

5. Because the Deeper Magic from before the Dawn of Time said that if an innocent person willingly gave up his life for a traitor, as Aslan did for Edmund, then the Stone Table would crack, and Time would start working backwards.

6. An Apple, with which to plant the Tree of Protection.

7. He chose Digory because it was Digory who was responsible for bringing Jadis into Narnia.

8. Emeth (in *The Last Battle*).

9. Hwin (in *The Horse and His Boy*).

10. It led to the South Sea Island where the people of Telmar had originally come from; and back into our own world (in *Prince Caspian*).

11. Edmund.

12. At the Stone Table.

13. Mr Beaver.

14. He asked Eustace to pierce his paw with a thorn. The blood from Aslan's paw made the dead King Caspian young again (in *The Silver Chair*).

15. The allies of the White Witch at the Stone Table.

16. Emeth.

17. Bury them.

18. So that they would get to know him better in our world.

19. Bree.

20. Rabadash.

The Silver Chair / 3 – page 48

1. People quarrelled, just as Jill and Eustace did when they quarrelled about what weapons they should carry before they set off on their quest to find the Lost Prince.

2. Giants.

3. They *didn't* throw boulders at them. Jill, Eustace and Puddleglum just got in the way when the stupid Giants were playing a game of cock-shies, which they played most nice mornings.

4. Harfang.

5. Eustace. (Carter and Spivvins were pupils at Experiment House, the school Eustace and Jill attended.)

6. Because the Giants at Harfang closed and locked their doors shortly after noon.

7. The letters spelling the words UNDER ME which were written on the stones of the old Giants' city and made up one of the four signs Aslan had given to Jill.

8. Puddleglum, after he had become tipsy in Harfang.

9. Aslan, who reminded her of the signs which she had forgotten.

10. He was surprised because he hadn't realized that humans' (and March-wiggles') faces were blue. (As Jill pointed out they were only blue from the cold.)

11. Man. (Marsh-wiggles like Puddleglum, however, were considered to be stringy and to have a muddy flavour.)

12. He had overheard the Giant who had killed the Stag remembering that the Stag had told him that he would be too tough to eat.

13. The Lady of the Green Kirtle, the Witch who had enchanted Prince Rilian and who had killed Prince Rilian's mother.

14. They were the words of the third sign that Aslan had told Jill she must obey.

15. That the Giant intended to eat them for their Autumn Feast.

16. Jill.

17. In the Underland.

18. The Giant Queen at Harfang.

19. After most of the Giants had gone off hunting, they sneaked out through an open door. When they were spotted they fell through a hole in the ground and into the Underland.

20. The Warden of the Marches of the Underland.

The Horse and His Boy / 3 – page 50

1. Narnia.

2. Queen Susan. He wanted to marry her, but she refused.

3. Aravis's father, Kidrash Tarkaan.

4. Mr Tumnus.

5. By the Tombs of the Ancient Kings.

6. Three Red Dwarf brothers who made an exhausted Shasta breakfast when he first arrived in Narnia.

7. He got into a fight in Tashbaan with a boy and his brothers who had made a cruel joke about Queen Susan.

8. Prince Corin.

9. Lasaraleen.

10. A wise Raven who came with King Edmund and Queen Susan to Tashbaan.

11. Because she was a Calormene.

12. She was hiding underneath a divan in the Old Palace when she overheard Rabadash telling his plans to the Tisroc and the Grand Vizier.

13. They pretended that they were preparing to hold a grand banquet on their galleon, the *Splendour Hyaline*. Once they were all aboard they would then sail off from Tashbaan and return to Narnia. (The plan was Mr Tumnus's idea.)

14. In the Old Palace in Tashbaan. They passed through these halls, as Aravis made her escape from Tashbaan.

15. King Lune.

16. Anvard guarded the pass that led into Narnia. Anyone who controlled the castle at Anvard would easily be able to invade Narnia.

17. Because they couldn't hear or repeat the secret plans of the Tisroc and his men.

18. She took her by the water-gate and led her to a punt down the river.

19. He planned to forge a letter from Susan saying that she was happy being with Rabadash.

20. Aslan.

The Magician's Nephew / 3 – page 52

1. The arrival of Jadis in London.

2. Aunt Letty.

3. She demanded that he find her a flying carpet, a chariot or a dragon.

4. He went out to order her a cab.

5. Now that Jadis had arrived in London, Sarah had never seen so much excitement before in her life.

6. Apart from all the chaos she would cause, he was worried that the sight of Jadis might frighten his sick mother to death.

7. The Cabby.

8. A hansom cab.

9. She threatened to destroy it.

10. A cross-bar which she had wrenched off an iron lamp-post.

11. The Cabby, Uncle Andrew and Strawberry, the horse.

12. She would feel weak and ill.

13. To an empty and dark world, which Jadis described as 'Nothing'. This was the world that was to become the world of Narnia.

14. The Cabby. Either that, or he thought they might all have died.

15. Uncle Andrew.

16. The cross-bar she had pulled off the lamp-post. It hit Aslan straight between the eyes.

17. It grew into a lamp-post.

18. The lamp-post became the lamp-post in Lantern Waste which marked the western boundary of Narnia, and which guided Lucy, Edmund, Peter and Susan into Narnia in *The Lion, the Witch and the Wardrobe*.

19. He planned to 'plant' the scrap metal in the soil of Narnia, and grow battleships and railway engines for nothing.

20. The Cabby. He sang everyone a harvest festival song to cheer them all up when they first arrived in Narnia.

Archenland – page 54

1. Narnia is to the north of Archenland and Calormen is to the south.

2. Cor (Shasta) and Aravis.

3. Because Shasta was fair-skinned, unlike the Calormenes who were dark-skinned.

4. Corin.

5. It was a mountain on the Narnia–Archenland border. People said that it was from here that bad weather always came to Archenland.

6. The Hermit of the Southern March.

7. It had been a Giant, who had been turned to stone.

8. Two brothers who fought Prince Rabadash and his army at the siege of Anvard.

9. Shasta.

10. King Nain.

11. The River Winding Arrow.

12. He was arrested by the Watch of the city after he had got into a fight defending the honour of Queen Susan. He escaped by getting the Watch drunk with wine.

13. Prince Rabadash's attack on Anvard and his attempted invasion of Archenland.

14. It was a former Talking Bear that had gone back to its wild ways. Corin found it and boxed it for thirty-three rounds until it saw the error of its ways!

15. Aravis.

16. Because he was the exact double of Prince Corin (which was hardly surprising because Shasta and Corin were twin brothers).

17. King Lune.

18. Tor. A brother's name was very often his older brother's name with an 'in' added on the end (for example Cor and Corin, Cole and Colin, and Dar and Darrin).

19. Pire, the Giant (who he turned into stone).

20. Corin did not want to become King, and the fact that Cor was born before him meant that he never would.

General / 6 – page 56

1. The crew of the *Dawn Treader.*

2. During the reign of King Tirian.

3. Peter, Susan, Edmund and Lucy.

4. Caspian.

5. Green.

6. Tarva (he was a star).

7. (a) Bism.

8. After dinner with Mr and Mrs Beaver, the Pevensie children heard about Aslan for the first time, and discovered that Edmund had gone missing.

9. Edmund and Lucy. (They appear in *The Lion, the Witch and the Wardrobe*, *Prince Caspian*, *The Voyage of the Dawn Treader*, *The Horse and His Boy* and *The Last Battle*.)

10. Roonwit the Centaur.

11. (c) She was sent to the House of Commons where she became a politician.

12. Because Dragons like nothing more than eating each other.

13. Giant Wimbleweather.

14. (a) King Miraz; (b) King Cor (Shasta); (c) King Frank.

15. The Hermit of the Southern March.

16. The Dark Island.

17. Trumpkin in *Prince Caspian* and Bree in *The Horse and His Boy*.

18. (a) *The Magician's Nephew*; (b) *The Lion, the Witch and the Wardrobe*; (c) *The Silver Chair*; (d) *Prince Caspian*; (e) *The Horse and His Boy*; (f) *The Voyage of the Dawn Treader*; (g) *The Last Battle*.

19. Her sewing machine.

20. (a) King Miraz; (b) Harold (Eustace's father); (c) Andrew.

The Last Battle / 3 – page 58

1. The Dwarfs.

2. Tashlan.

3. Poggin. Eustace also taught the Dwarf the names of the animals and plants from our world.

4. Aunt Polly.

5. That the Calormenes had taken over Cair Paravel, and that Roonwit the Centaur was dead.

6. A Narnian weed that looks like wood-sorrel but tastes much better, especially with butter and pepper.

7. They decided that they had been fooled for too long and that they had no more time for any more fake Aslans, or any Kings and Queens. From now on, they decided that the Dwarfs would be just for the Dwarfs.

8. Poggin.

9. The Talking Dogs.

10. Lantern Waste.

11. All the small Talking Beasts who could nibble away at the Horses' bonds to set them free.

12. The Dwarfs.

13. Archenland.

14. A noble man of Calormen who Aslan allowed into his own country.

15. He planned to saw off the Unicorn's horn and make him pull a cart.

16. The Dwarfs. That was the name the Calormenes called them.

17. Lagour.

18. He was thrown into the Stable by King Tirian where he was destroyed by Aslan.

19. When he entered the Stable and saw Tash. He was so frightened that he forgot how to speak and was never seen again.

20. Jill and Eustace, and the High King Peter, King Edmund and Queen Lucy, and Lord Digory and Lady Polly.

The Lion, the Witch and the Wardrobe / 4 – page 59

1. She would make Peter a Duke, and she would make Susan and Lucy Duchesses.

2. Cair Paravel.

3. To the Witch's house.

4. To the Stone Table to meet with Aslan.

5. Edmund betrayed them all to her, and told her that Aslan had come back to Narnia.

6. He gave Peter a golden sword and a silver shield. Susan was given a bow and arrows, and an ivory horn that could summon help in times of great danger. Lucy's presents were a small dagger and a tiny diamond bottle, which contained a magic cordial made from one of the fire-berries of the Sun and which could heal any illness.

7. When the others met Father Christmas he was at the Witch's house.

8. Father Christmas left a sewing-machine back at the Beavers' house for Mrs Beaver, and he mended Mr Beaver's dam and fitted a new sluice-gate.

9. For Peter, Edmund, Susan and Lucy.

10. Her reign and her life would end.

11. Mr Beaver showed them the handkerchief which Mr Tumnus had given Lucy, and which the Faun had given to the Beaver shortly before he was arrested.

12. Dry bread and water.

13. Aslan.

14. Susan with her horn.

15. By killing Maugrim, the Wolf.

16. Because according to the Deep Magic every traitor's life was hers by rights.

17. Peter, after he had killed the Wolf.

18. The side of the White Witch.

19. On the Stone Table.

20. The house of the White Witch.

Prince Caspian / 4 – page 61

1. He helped Aslan spread the news of the Telmarines' defeat.

2. Pattertwig.

3. The Bulgy Bears.

4. They were terrified by the Walking Trees who Aslan had awoken from their long sleep.

5. Trumpkin.

6. He wanted to kill him.

7. He said that they could either stay and live in peace with the Old Narnians, or return from the world they had originally come from.

8. One of the Bulgy Bears; the Giant Wimbleweather; and Glenthorn the Centaur.

9. The Bulgy Bear.

10. He said that, as some Humans are afraid of Mice, it wouldn't have been fair on King Miraz.

11. No one is quite certain but it seems very likely that her obnoxious schoolchildren were turned into pigs. (Certainly the children were never seen again, but there were a lot of new pigs in that area that no one had spotted before.)

12. Peter.

13. Doctor Cornelius.

14. Because they were Humans. (They were descended from pirates who had originally come from our world through one of the few 'chinks' which still exist between our world and the world of Narnia.)

15. The sound of Queen Susan's magic horn being blown.

16. Aslan thought Caspian would be a worthy King of Narnia precisely because Caspian thought he wasn't worthy.

17. A Hedgehog.

18. He sent them off on a mission to discover new lands beyond the Eastern Ocean. (When he became King, Caspian sailed off in the *Dawn Treader* to find these Lords.)

19. They were both too old.

20. Aslan sent them back through the Door in the Air he had made.

The Talking Beasts of Narnia / 2 – page 63

1. Wolves.

2. He used his tail for balance.

3. Glimfeather, the Owl.

4. Fledge.

5. He asked them to be kind to them, but never to return to their ways.

6. King Frank and Queen Helen.

7. The Beavers.

8. Horses. Hwin was the only Talking Horse.

9. He was a winged Horse.

10. They stopped being Talking Beasts and were never seen again.

11. Field-mice, who later became Talking Mice.

12. An Eagle.

13. Shift the Ape.

14. Because they knew a lot of the same people and places.

15. Food and drink.

16. Bears.

17. To Calormen, on Aslan's orders. ('Aslan' was, of course, Puzzle in disguise.)

18. A Squirrel.

19. The High King Peter.

20. To lose the ability to talk.

General / 7 – page 65

1. (a) Corin; (b) Dar; (c) Edmund.

2. The daughter of the Chief Dufflepud, who spoke the spell that made the Dufflepuds invisible in the first place.

3. In the Last Sea.

4. In *The Last Battle* at the end of Narnia.

5. (c) At a railway station.

6. The Giants of Harfang.

7. Digory.

8. The Talking Beasts of Narnia (they had mistaken Uncle Andrew for some sort of plant).

9. (a) Tirian, Jill and Eustace in *The Last Battle*; (b) Puzzle in *The Last Battle*; (c) the Queen of Underland in *The Silver Chair*; (d) Shasta and Aravis in *The Horse and His Boy*.

10. Professor Kirke in *The Lion, the Witch and the Wardrobe* when they came to him and told him how worried they were about Lucy and her stories of Narnia.

11. Father Time.

12. (d) Ilkeen is a great lake in Calormen.

13. In *The Voyage of the Dawn Treader* when the ship was sailing towards the end of the world.

14. (a) Peter's, Susan's, Edmund's and Lucy's (Alberta was Eustace's mother); (b) Digory's; (c) Prince Caspian's.

15. The North Star.

16. Mr Tumnus.

17. The Queen of Underland and her servants.

18. Golg and the People of Bism. When the Queen of Underland was killed, they left the Shallow Lands, where they had been living as slaves, and returned to the Really Deep lands.

19. (a) Trufflehunter.

20. (b) Stonefoot is a Giant and all the others are Dwarfs.

The Voyage of the Dawn Treader / 4 – page 67

1. Aslan.

2. A former star who had retired and who Caspian and the crew of the *Dawn Treader* met.

3. The missing Lords Argoz, Mavramorn and Revilian.

4. In an argument one of them had picked up a knife from the table. What none of them knew was that the knife was the Knife of Stone, the knife the White Witch had used to kill Aslan on the Stone Table hundreds of years ago, and they fell under its enchantment.

5. Only if Caspian and the others sailed to the World's End, and then returned, leaving one of their crew behind, would the Lords ever wake up.

6. A fire-berry from the valleys of the Sun.

7. Sleep – without any dreams.

8. Caspian.

9. The Dawn Treaders were all those crew members who agreed to leave Ramandu's Island and travel with Caspian to the World's End.

10. He was the only member of Caspian's crew who refused to travel on to the World's End.

11. The Sea People.

12. The seawater turned sweet.

13. Caspian.

14. The Silver Sea.

15. Aslan.

16. Because he knew that there was the danger that some of his men would fall in love with the Sea People and dive overboard to join them.

17. A Lamb.

18. Aslan.

19. Edmund and Lucy.

20. They said it was the fault of the Pevensie children.

The Silver Chair / 4 – page 69

1. Man.

2. She wanted him to help her rule over Narnia.

3. The subjects of the Witch of the Underland.

4. She was busy supervising the digging that would shortly create an entry into the surface lands.

5. To the surface.

6. Old Father Time. (They saw him again in *The Last Battle*, at the very end of Narnia.)

7. The Earthmen, the subjects of the Witch.

8. Prince Rilian.

9. Underground. Bism was the Really Deep Land that existed below the Shallow Lands, and was the home of the gnomes who had been put under an enchantment by the Witch.

10. He would become mad and destroy anyone he could.

11. He would become free of the Witch's magic, and remember who he really was.

12. The Queen of Underland with her enchantments.

13. Prince Rilian, as soon as Jill, Eustace and Puddleglum had freed him.

14. He put out the fire that the Witch had lit, because the smoke from it was making them fall under her magic spells.

15. Prince Rilian and Puddleglum. (Eustace also attacked her, but his sword didn't even get through her scales.)

16. As they left the Dark Castle after the Witch had been killed and Underland was being destroyed.

17. The Witch had prepared a series of magic spells that meant that her entire kingdom would be destroyed if she was ever killed.

18. The Great Winter Dance that happens the first night in Narnia when the moon is bright and the ground is snowy.

19. The Healing of Harms was when Aslan welcomed the dead King Caspian into his own country and made him young again.

20. That he might travel to Jill and Eustace's world for just a few minutes.

The Horse and His Boy / 4 – page 71

1. The Hermit of the Southern March.

2. Because he believed that Narnia was protected by a terrible demon who took the form of a Lion.

3. Aslan.

4. He was too busy in the North fighting the Giants there.

5. He saw everything that was happening in the world in the reflection of a Pool.

6. Ahoshta – the man she was supposed to have married.

7. They rolled in the grass.

8. Because Princes, not Kings, have all the fun.

9. A lion (in reality it was Aslan).

10. The ten scratches were Aravis's punishment for drugging her serving-maid when she made her escape from her father's house. The scratches on her back were the same number as the number of whip-lashes the slave had received when it was discovered that Aravis had disappeared. (The lion was, of course, Aslan.)

11. He was ashamed of not having run back to try and save Aravis from the lion.

12. The Hermit of the Southern March. He told Bree that all he had lost was his self-conceit.

13. They used a huge tree-trunk as a battering ram.

14. He managed to warn King Lune in time about Rabadash's plans to attack Anvard.

15. He was killed by King Lune.

16. A donkey (and not a talking Donkey either). Following Aslan's advice he went to the altar of Tash during the Autumn Feast where he became human again – unfortunately the whole of Tashbaan saw that he had once been a donkey and he became a figure of fun.

17. Because he knew that if he went further than ten miles away from Tashbaan he would become a donkey again. And because he didn't dare send anyone else to fight wars for him and win the fame which would make them more popular then himself, he became the most peaceable Tisroc Calormen had ever known.

18. When he learnt that Aslan was a real Lion after all.

19. Prince Corin.

20. So they could carry on arguing and making peace more conveniently.

Reepicheep – page 73

1. Aslan made then all Talking Mice as thanks after their ancestors had chewed away at his cords at the Stone Table.

2. He wanted to travel eastwards to the end of the world and to see Aslan's country.

3. Eustace.

4. He fell overboard and discovered that the seawater was sweet instead of salty.

5. He would keep him company at nights and tell him tales of people who had fallen on hard times but who had nevertheless got better and lived happily ever after.

6. Where the sky and water met, and where the waves grow sweet.

7. The second-in-command of the Talking Mice of Narnia.

8. Reep.

9. Prince Caspian.

10. A coracle.

11. Pug.

12. Eustace.

13. Because he always played the game as if it was a real battle, and would send his knights into dangerous situations.

14. Pick him up in her arms and hug him. She finally did so when she said goodbye to him at the end of *The Voyage of the Dawn Treader*.

15. Eustace.

16. The second battle of Beruna.

17. A gold coronet and a red feather.

18. When Reepicheep's tail had been cut off, they offered to cut off their own tails, as they didn't want their leader to be the only Talking Mouse in Narnia without a tail. (Aslan, of course, restored Reepicheep's tail.)

19. When he approached Aslan's country.

20. In *The Last Battle* when they returned to Narnia for the final time.

The Magician's Nephew / 4 – page 74

1. By Aslan's song – they appeared from out of the very earth of Narnia.

2. They became Talking Beasts. The large animals also became a little smaller and the small ones grew a little larger.

3. Jadis. (The animals had misheard Aslan when he called Jadis 'an evil'.)

4. Aslan made him into a flying horse so that he could take Digory and Polly on their journey to bring an Apple back for Aslan.

5. The Jackdaw. Although the Jackdaw thought that he had made the First Joke, Aslan pointed out that he had, in fact, been the First Joke, when he had drawn attention to himself by speaking loudly when everyone else had finished talking.

6. Uncle Andrew. They finally decided that he was a tree and tried to plant him.

7. He wanted Aslan to give him something magic to make his sick mother well again.

8. Aslan ordered Digory to travel far beyond the Western Waste and bring back an Apple from which Aslan wanted to plant a tree that would protect Narnia. (Later, Aslan allowed Digory to take an apple from the tree to bring to his mother.)

9. Digory, Polly, Uncle Andrew and the Cabby.

10. Brandy.

11. The Cabby and his wife, Nellie, who became King Frank and Queen Helen.

12. They planted it, and in the morning it had grown into a small toffee tree.

13. She tried to persuade him to take an Apple back for his mother, and not give it to Aslan, who, she claimed, only wanted it for himself.

14. For years it protected Narnia from Jadis, who would never dare to come within a hundred miles of the tree.

15. Digory.

16. Dwarfs.

17. A golden tree that had grown from the gold sovereigns that had fallen out of Uncle Andrew's pockets.

18. She ate the Apple of Life that Digory had taken, with Aslan's permission, from the Tree of Protection.

19. They buried them in Digory's back garden.

20. He had part of it made into a wardrobe. Many years later, Lucy, Edmund, Peter and Susan would discover Narnia when they entered the very same wardrobe in *The Lion, the Witch and the Wardrobe*.

The Last Battle / 4 – page 76

1. Emeth.

2. He was destroyed by Tash.

3. Aslan.

4. The High King Peter.

5. Clean their swords.

6. Susan.

7. 'Boys' or 'girls'.

8. Tash.

9. Because all the good things that Emeth had done in his life in the service of Tash had really been done in Aslan's name. Nothing good can ever be done in Tash's name.

10. Old Father Time.

11. They stopped being Talking Beasts, passed off to Aslan's left, into his shadow, and were never seen or heard of again.

12. Dragons and Giant Lizards.

13. Old Father Time.

14. Reepicheep.

15. Emeth.

16. Because this was the real Narnia. The Narnia they had known before had just been a shadow and a pale imitation of the real Narnia.

17. Mr Tumnus.

18. Professor Kirke's (Digory's).

19. The world we live in.

20. The Stable on Stable Hill, and also the garden Aslan had led them all to after they had passed through the Stable door.

General / 8 – page 78

1. The war that freed Narnia from the rule of King Miraz and his New Narnians.

2. (d) Lantern Waste.

3. They were both teachers.

4. The White Witch.

5. Overworld was the surface world, above the Underland.

6. Coriakin.

7. Trumpkin.

8. By Magic.

9. Duffle, Rogin and Bricklethumb.

10. Aslan.

11. (a) Seven Dwarfs who helped Prince Caspian; (b) the seven good friends of Caspian's father who the evil King Miraz sent into exile; (c) a group of islands to the east of Narnia. Two of the islands were called Muil and Brenn.

12. (a) *Prince Caspian*; (b) *The Lion, the Witch and the Wardrobe*; (c) *The Voyage of the Dawn Treader*; (d) *The Silver Chair*; (e) *The Magician's Nephew*; (f) *The Horse and His Boy*; (g) *The Last Battle*.

13. (a) Aslan; (b) Lucy found Narnia in the Wardrobe; (c) in the Lone Islands, Caspian freed all the slaves and ended slavery there for ever; (d) to find Prince Rilian of Narnia; (e) he took Jill and Eustace to fetch an apple for Aslan; (f) Queen Susan and King Edmund; (g) Jill and Eustace came from our world to help King Tirian.

14. Digory (Professor Kirke).

15. Being a King or a Queen in Narnia.

16. Lucy, Edmund, Eustace and Reepicheep (Caspian had already been bought as a slave by the Lord Bern).

17. Jadis.

18. Eustace.

19. He had been expecting to meet great warriors and not children.

20. (d) Harfang.

The Lion, the Witch and the Wardrobe / 5 – page 80

1. That the life of any traitor belongs to the White Witch.

2. They disguised themselves as a tree-stump and a boulder.

3. Father Christmas.

4. Narnia would be destroyed.

5. Her magic wand that could turn people to stone.

6. Aslan.

7. Leopards.

8. Susan and Lucy.

9. The White Witch and her army.

10. Aslan.

11. It said that if someone who had committed no crime himself sacrificed his life freely for the life of a traitor, then the Stone Table would crack and Time itself would start working backwards. That is how Aslan returned from the 'dead' after he had been killed by the White Witch, for he had offered up his own life for the life of Edmund.

12. Susan and Lucy.

13. She intended to kill Edmund anyway.

14. Field-mice.

15. Susan and Lucy.

16. It cracked, as the Deeper Magic said it would, because Aslan had given up his own innocent life for the life of a traitor.

17. A ghost.

18. Romping with Aslan after he had come back from the dead.

19. To the Witch's house.

20. After the final battle with the White Witch.

The Land of Calormen – page 81

1. Archenland.

2. Tash.

3. King Tirian with Jill and Eustace in *The Last Battle*. They dressed up in Calormene mail, and darkened their faces with juice from a bottle.

4. The Tisroc.

5. Tashbaan, the capital of Calormen.

6. The Bight of Calormen was the bay on the eastern shore of Calormen.

7. Rishda Tarkaan.

8. They were two Calormene gods. (Zardeenah was also known as the Lady of the Night and of Maidens.)

9. Their captives and slaves. Tirian, Jill and Eustace rescued a group of Dwarfs who had been captured by the Calormenes and were on their way to the salt-pits.

10. It is a coin, and is one-fortieth of a crescent.

11. Bree, when he was still a captured Horse in Calormen. (Of course, his Calormene master didn't know that Bree was really a Talking Horse.)

12. (c) Gwendolen. All the others are natives of Calormen. Gwendolen was a Narnian schoolgirl who joined Aslan in *Prince Caspian*.

13. The Calormene custom of saying 'may he live for ever' whenever they mention the Tisroc's name.

14. Rabadash.

15. King Edmund and Queen Susan.

16. Aravis's father.

17. A scimitar.

18. The Valley of a Thousand Perfumes.

19. His senior officer. That was the name by which the senior officers of Calormene soldiers were always referred to by junior officers.

20. They attacked the royal castle with a fleet of twenty ships.

Out and About in Narnia and Beyond – page 82

1. Narnia.

2. (a) deep beneath Narnia in the Underland; (b) at the eastern edge of the world; (c) also underneath Narnia.

3. The White Witch.

4. In the Bight of Calormen at the beginning of the eastern sea, just off the coast of Archenland.

5. Professor Kirke in *The Lion, the Witch and the Wardrobe*.

6. At the eastern edge of Lantern Waste.

7. Seven Dwarf-brothers.

8. The River Rush.

9. Marsh-wiggles.

10. Bism.

11. It was a deserted island visited by the *Dawn Treader*, and lay between Dragon Island and Deathwater Island.

12. Beaversdam.

13. Atlantis.

14. In the west, far beyond Lantern Waste.

15. Avra.

16. They were given to Narnia by the Lone Islanders themselves after King Gale, who was ninth in descent from King Frank, had defeated a Dragon.

17. Calormen.

18. Uncle Andrew in *The Magician's Nephew*.

19. Aslan's How.

20. The world of Narnia was flat. Our world, of course, is round.

General / 9 – page 84

1. (a) In Calormen.

2. In the Magician's Book on the Island of the Dufflepuds.

3. They were all Fauns who met up with Prince Caspian on Dancing Lawn.

4. Constellations.

5. Shift the Ape in *The Last Battle*.

6. High King Peter and King Caspian (Prince Caspian).

7. Slinky was a Fox and Wraggle was a Satyr.

8. (d) A white Stag.

9. Mr Tumnus.

10. Moonwood the Hare.

11. (a) Rhindon.

12. At Experiment House. Cholmondley Major was one of the pupils there.

13. Fair Olvin.

14. (a) Lucy Pevensie. All the others were pupils at Experiment House.

15. Reepicheep.

16. Harold and Alberta, Eustace's parents.

17. (a) Corradin. He fought with Rabadash at the siege of Anvard and was killed by King Edmund.

18. The High King Peter.

19. So that they should get to know him better in their own world.

20. They died in a railway accident and Aslan brought them to his own world.

The Lion, the Witch and the Wardrobe / 6 – page 86

1. The White Witch when she was better known as Jadis in *The Magician's Nephew*.

2. The statues of all the creatures the White Witch had turned into stone.

3. Because she was descended from Lilith who was a Jinn and Adam's first wife, before Eve.

4. He breathed on them.

5. Aslan. (He carried them on his back.)

6. Rumblebuffin.

7. Her handkerchief.

8. Edmund.

9. A red lion.

10. All the creatures who had been statues in the Witch's house and who had been brought back to life by Aslan.

11. Aslan.

12. Lucy.

13. Because he was the oldest.

14. At Cair Paravel.

15. (a) Susan the Gentle; (b) Peter the Magnificent; (c) Lucy the Valiant; and (d) Edmund the Just.

16. Mr Tumnus.

17. In the west of Narnia, near Lantern Waste and the lamp-post.

18. It led them back to the lamp-post.

19. Three servants of Professor Kirke.

20. By the odd things they said, or the look they had in their eyes.

The Life and Works of C.S. Lewis – page 88

1. Clive Staples.

2. Jack.

3. He was born in Belfast in Northern Ireland on 29th November 1898.

4. Mr Tumnus, a Faun carrying parcels and an umbrella.

5. He taught at Oxford University from 1925 until 1954, when he moved to Cambridge University.

6. J.R.R. Tolkien who wrote *The Hobbit* and *The Lord of the Rings*.

7. Animal-Land, in the fictional world of Boxen.

8. Aslan. Later Lewis would say that he started dreaming of Lions – and that is how Aslan came to be in *The Lion, the Witch and the Wardrobe* and all the other stories.

9. Screwtape is a devil, and *The Screwtape Letters* are the letters he writes to his nephew, in which he tells him about the best ways to tempt mankind to sin.

10. *The Last Battle*.

11. The three books are *Out of the Silent Planet*, *Perelandra*, and *That Hideous Strength*.

12. *Shadowlands*. (The play was written by the dramatist William Nicholson.)

13. Lewis said that he based the character of Puddleglum on his gardener, Paxford.

14. Pauline Baynes.

15. The Inklings were a group of friends who met at Oxford University during the 1930s and the 1940s to talk about literature and writing. Lewis was a member of this group, as was his friend J.R.R. Tolkien.

16. He let a group of children come to live with him at The Kilns, his home in the country, to escape the bombs that were falling on London at the time.

17. These were the original names for Peter, Susan, Edmund and Lucy.

18. J.R.R. Tolkien.

19. *The Silver Chair*.

20. In 1963.